# Contents

# Introduction

There are 10 commandments in the Bible. Far too many for some people, not nearly enough for others.

Jesus reduced the 10 to 2 and wrapped them in one word. Love.

Sounds simple, doesn't it? Well . . . doesn't it?

As a matter of fact—no!

There are so many tough questions in our complex world that don't have easy answers. At least we haven't found them. And we've been looking, trying to find the proper Christian response to issues like

> world hunger
> capital punishment
> equality for women
> divorce, and many others.

This book takes a careful look at 13 key questions Christians can't dodge. We face them in the voting booth, the grocery store, at home, and at church. So, these debates are important to us.

To help us sharpen our thinking, we've pitted 26 Christian experts against each other. Two competent scholars have developed the case for and against each of the 13 statements for debate. Some writers have agreed to present arguments they do not entirely support. They have done this for the sake of getting both sides of the issues before us; we are grateful to Clayton Bonar and Robert Hubbard for helping us in this way.

And so, in the spirit of Christian love, and with a prayer for spiritual insight, we turn to Christians debating 13 tough issues.

# No Easy Answers:

## *Christians Debate Today's Issues*

**Stephen M. Miller**
Editor

**Mary Jo Van Dyne**
Editorial Assistant

**Photo, Art Credits**

Cover: Comstock

Pages 43, 70, back cover: Reprinted with permission from The Saturday Evening Post Society, a division of BFL&MS, Inc., © 1984.

Page 96: Copyright 1984, Universal Press Syndicate. Reprinted with permission. All rights reserved.

Page 25, Black Star; page 33, H. Armstrong Roberts; page 52, Israel Ministry of Tourism; page 104, William Koechling; page 113, The Costas

The following versions of Scripture have been used by permission:

All Bible quotations are taken from *The Holy Bible, New International Version* (NIV) unless otherwise noted. Copyright © 1978 by the New York International Bible Society.

The *New American Standard Bible* (NASB), © The Lockman Foundation, 1960, 1962, 1963, 1968, 1971, 1972, 1973, 1975, 1977.

The *New King James Version* (NKJV), copyright © 1979, 1980, 1982, Thomas Nelson, Inc., Publishers.

The *Revised Standard Version of the Bible* (RSV), copyrighted 1946, 1952, © 1971, 1973.

The King James Version (KJV).

ISBN: 083-411-0652

# No
# Easy
# Answers
Christians Debate Today's Issues

Published for the ALDERSGATE ASSOCIATES
Copyright 1985
Beacon Hill Press of Kansas City
Kansas City, Missouri
Printed in the United States of America

# Other Dialog Series Books

For a description of all available Dialog Series books,
including some that may not be listed here,
contact your publishing house
and ask for the free Dialog Series brochure.

## Chapter 1

*The Issue:*

# Soul Winning

*Statement for Debate:*

### Every Christian must be a soul winner.

by

Jack Hawthorne (For)

Randall E. Davey (Against)

*Background Scripture:*

### Matthew 28:16-20; Acts 8:1-4; 1 Corinthians 3:6-9

Lᴇᴛ'ꜱ ʙᴇɢɪɴ this debate by looking at some of the words in the statement we're debating, and

> **FOR**

let's first face that sticky word *must.* If it is a must that comes from some impelling force that drives us to seek divine acceptance through such efforts, we would have to step back and unmask this activity as an attempt to earn salvation by works. But for this brief debate, let's associate this word with the motivation of love for both a lost world and a concerned Heavenly Father.

The term *every* obviously leaves out no one. We're not saying that each person would be equally gifted as a soul winner, but that all of God's children have this opportunity. While some are more gifted than others, in reality those who are full of the Spirit strongly draw men to Christ. And who can bear such fruit? Every Christian.

The term *Christian* has certainly been debated by many groups. But for this discussion, let's agree that a Christian is a person who accepts Jesus Christ as Savior from sin's power, yields completely to His Lordship, and allows that relationship to determine his life-style.

When we use the term *soul winner* we are not implying that some mortal has been able to reach into another man's heart and make some immortal change. But we are saying that mortals can proclaim, describe, and illustrate the gospel, which is "the power of God for salvation" (Romans 1:16, NASB). Jesus assured His followers that they would receive power to be witnesses. This promise in Acts 1:8 is not limited to only a few, but is the assurance of enablement for all those who receive the Holy Spirit. This power isn't a "gift of gab"—it is the result of God's love flowing through us as open channels. Today I was told of a fearful young lady impelled by the Spirit to witness to a friend who had rejected Christ many times. Instead of her well-planned presentation the young lady could only weep and tell her friend she loved her and wanted her to no longer reject God's love. It was not eloquence of words, but the eloquence of love that melted her friend's heart and brought her to repentance.

Now let me tell you why I believe every Christian must be a soul winner:

*1. Because God "has committed to us the word of reconciliation. Therefore, we are ambassadors for Christ" (2 Corinthians*

"However . . . don't get the idea that I'm trying to convert you."

*5:19-20, NASB).* I do not believe God commissions His official ambassadors with a noneffective message. Rather, every Christian is given the responsibility of being God's agent to bring His love to any who are separated from Him—and God guarantees that such a mission is backed by His authority.

2. *Because Jesus commanded it.* Matthew 28:19-20 is a directive for Christians to go out and make spiritual behavior changes; that is, "teaching [men] to observe all that was commanded" (NASB). Men cannot observe all Jesus commanded without that spiritual miracle of being born again, can they? It is clear that Jesus expected us to go and teach in a manner that produces a life change, because He planned to go along as the power Source.

The Early Church understood that every believer was to be a proclaimer. Notice Acts 8:1 (NASB), "they were all scattered throughout the regions of Judea and Samaria, except the apostles." Notice especially who went out ("all"), and in verse 4 what they did: they "preached the word!" It was not just the apostles, or the gifted ones—they all went. And they all shared Christ. Even the humble, Spirit-filled table-keeper, Philip, could see a mass movement to Christ in Samaria. And he took part in an effective personal witness on the lonely Gaza road.

3. *Because Jesus set that example.* He loved a lost world, and His mission was to seek that which was lost. He did not come merely to let the world see His exemplary life, but to save that world. If I follow His example, I'll live in a manner that not only lets men see Jesus in my life, but that also tells those men exactly how they can find the same peace and joy that I am exhibiting. I heard Dr. James Kennedy tell of a classmate in his high school who was attractively different, and Jim wanted desperately to be like him, but he didn't know how. Much later he learned the boy was a Christian. In his silence, the classmate's eloquent witness was only about *himself.* Living the life is important, but it is not enough.

4. *Because Jesus put His love within us.* Romans 5:5 (NASB) says: "Because the love of God has been poured out within our hearts through the Holy Spirit who was given to us." I believe the "must" is there in my heart because His love is

within me and because that love is a soul-winning kind of love.

Jesus' love motivated Him to pay a tremendous price. Christians can also pay a price and become soul winners by the "must" of love, without the legalistic "gotta go." Part of that price can come in the form of seeking instruction by effective soul winners who can teach us how to lead others to Christ. Such programs include Dr. Kennedy's Evangelism Explosion. And part of the price is paid when we go and love and reach out to the lost and hurting with compassion, like the Good Samaritan did.

What is the most important thing that ever happened to you? Isn't it that someone shared Jesus with you? What, then, is the most important thing you can do for someone else? Shouldn't it be to share Jesus in the power of the Spirit, and to leave the results with God, who said, "My word . . . shall not return to Me empty, without accomplishing what I desire, and without succeeding in the matter for which I sent it" (Isaiah 55:11, NASB)?

An unknown writer put it this way, "If when I trusted Christ to save me I was eligible for heaven, why am I still here? It must be to do the one thing I can do here that I can't do there!"

I TAKE ISSUE with folks who insist that every **AGAINST** Christian must be a soul winner.

Not for the sake of argument alone is the issue raised—but for the sake of many who suffer guilt and despair for not being able to cite even one lone convert after years of serving Christ and His Church.

It's for the sake of many who struggle to accept God's free gift of grace, who feel it's more reasonable to earn one's salvation, that this idea must be questioned.

It's for the sake of those who really do live by faith in the Son of God but at the same time battle feelings of inadequacy and indescribable fears, persons who don't need to register yet another failure by failing to "win one."

It's for those whose body has surrendered long before their mind or spirit, persons confined to beds, wheelchairs, or maximum-care facilities, believers who already wrestle with not being "doers of the Word." And, it's for the many members of Christ's "chosen race" who live in political and religious climates, hostile to Christianity, whose whispered witness may be sufficient to endanger their very lives.

To appreciate the fuss this subject generates, we need a clear understanding of terms. The irritating term is *soul winner*. The combination of those 10 letters brings more snakes to the surface than one can possibly kill in this limited space. But a few healthy swats are in order. The term *soul winner* is not to be confused with *witness* in any of its tenses. Most Christians are witnesses of one kind or another, but not all of them can or should be "soul winners."

First, to talk about one's soul—the apparent target of the "soul winner"—you have to engage in a complex dissection of man. Early church father, Origen, was one of the first to do such surgery. But he, along with one who followed centuries later, Martin Luther, preferred to talk about man as a complete entity having various dimensions. Controversy focuses over the proper definition of *soul,* and the burden belongs to those who do the dissecting and then go for man's soul as that part that needs redemption. Some of these folks discourage use of the term *soul* as that which needs grace. They prefer to talk about one's spirit. But, even if the term was *spirit winner,* the argument would be unhindered.

Second, the term *winner* quickly brings to mind the word *loser,* an all-too-familiar term with which everyone can easily identify. Both terms take on all kinds of baggage in capitalistic societies where winning is the dream of every man. Winning may mean recognition to one, wealth to another, or beating the home team to yet others. But underlying these sample meanings rests one's best effort with a capital *E*. The great stories of winners focus on long hours of practice, starting out at the "bottom," and the rough trek to success.

Given the various meanings, then, of *soul* and *winner,* one can see the dynamite and matches coming dangerously close. The obvious depersonalization ("I can't stand him ... but I love his soul"), and the need to score makes for some extremely insensitive monologue in the name of One who illustrated sensitivity as a way of life.

I suggest, then, that believers are not required to "win souls." In fact, the implied task is the ministry and work of the Holy Spirit who agrees to work with His many witnesses to see reconciliation between God and man. Such conclusions are obvious in the scriptures to which we turn for counsel. There, you would need to read a yet-discovered text to find *soul winner* anywhere. So, with a couple of snakes dead and a few more dazed, the Scripture offers its own kind of blow.

1. The familiar text of Acts 1:8 records, "But you will receive power when the Holy Spirit comes on you; and you will be my *witnesses* in Jerusalem, and in all Judea and Samaria, and to the ends of the earth" (emphasis added). *My witnesses* originally shared meaning with our word *martyrs.* The work of witness-bearing is similar in nature to "light bearing" in Isaiah 49:6, according to Bible commentator F. F. Bruce. Nowhere, however, does the term suggest that we are to go beyond giving an account or report of truth as we understand it. The witness, then, does not turn to the jury to present the "close."

2. In dealing with soul winning, reference is often cited from the Parable of the Great Supper found in Luke 14:23, "Then the master told his servant, 'Go out to the roads and country lanes and make them come in, so that my house will be full.'" Again, advocates of "soul winning" are driving up the wrong lane when they suggest this passage justifies the "anything goes, scare 'em with a gruesome illustration" tactic. Vincent, in his *Word Studies in the New Testament,* says the word *make* does not mean "to use force, but to constrain them against the reluctance which such poor creatures would feel at accepting the invitation of a great lord."

3. Help on the matter is found more specifically in 1 Corinthians 3:6-7, "I planted the seed, Apollos watered it, but God made it grow. So neither he who plants nor he who waters is anything, but only God, who makes things grow." Without question, God uses mortals in cooperation with His Holy Spirit. But "winners" in this context is not the right adjective.

Though we confess some snakes die hard, we would encourage the folks with whom we argue to press listeners to be faithful witnesses, obedient servants, and sensitive listeners. The soul winner's motives are admirable, but his claims are better left in a viper's pit.

## Reaction and Rebuttal

**M**Y OPPONENT HAS SAID that "believers are not required to win souls" and that the term *soul winner* is not biblical. But Proverbs 11:30 says, "He who is wise wins souls" (NASB).

| FOR |

In the economy of God, souls are of supreme value, and every Christian who truly follows the example of Christ will win those souls.

Discussion of whether we win souls or spirits is really irrelevant, for the bottom line is simply that we must bring men and women to a saving knowledge of Jesus Christ.

The issue is clearest to me as I read John 4 and sense the constraint of the love of Jesus—a love that is to fill and guide each Christian's life. In this passage, Jesus sought to win an outcast of the "Samaritan dogs." In verse 34, He said that His food was to do the Father's will (soul winning). In verse 35, Jesus said the people thought of harvest as four months away, but Jesus saw a "ripe harvest" now. In this context, "harvesting" can only mean "winning souls." In verse 36, Jesus saw that reapers in His harvest field were having a payday now as they gathered fruit for eternal life. That sounds like winning souls. In verse 39, the woman's testimony bore fruit, that is, souls were won. And all of us have His order that *we* are to bear the fruit that remains (John 15:16).

The constraint of His love puts a "must" in my soul until I am motivated by that love to see the value of winning those "pearls" so worthy of the great price He paid for them.

**I**'LL GRANT that the Bible does make it clear that Christians are to be "witnesses," "ambassa-

13

dors for Christ," and a "letter of Christ." But the Bible is not so precise concerning *how* we are to become all of these.

Those who say that every Christian must be a soul winner have handily worked their proof text with good intent, coupling with them "tools" for presentation of gospel truth. *The Four Spiritual Laws, Roman Road,* and *The Kennedy Plan* are but a few such tools that systematically link biblical truths with methods of delivery. Together, these lead would-be converts to an obvious conclusion. The "plans" are so sensible that a vast majority of people who hear the presentation may in fact respond favorably, without understanding the far-reaching extent of their response.

In James F. Engle's *Contemporary Christian Communications,* he quotes John Scott as saying, "We must never degrade evangelism into being merely or even mainly a technique to be learned or a formula to be recited."

E. M. Griffin, author of *The Mind Changers,* wrote, "Any persuasive effort which restricts another's freedom to choose for or against Jesus Christ . . . is nothing short of manipulation."

Engle himself rightly concludes, "Those who contend that Christian vitality is commensurate with individual evangelistic output are guilty of trying to make everyone into an eye or an ear. In short, they are assuming, in violation of Scripture, that all are to do the work of an evangelist."

It is the spirit of God who uses the verbal witness of one, the silent witness of another, and the works witness of yet another to draw the world to himself. He, the Potter, we the clay.

*Jack Hawthorne is a pastor in Flagstaff, Ariz.*

*Randall E. Davey is a pastor in Overland Park, Kans.*

## Chapter 2

*The Issue:*

# Christian Schools

*Statement for Debate:*

**Christians should support Christian schools, and where possible, enroll their children in them.**

by

Shegay Vanderpool (For)

Vern Houser (Against)

*Background Scripture:*

**Deuteronomy 6:1-7; Proverbs 22:6; Matthew 5:14-16**

$A$s PARENTS or teachers, we need to train our children as they *should* go rather than *would* go.

| FOR |
| --- |

We can quickly see this in Proverbs 22:6, "Train up a child in the way he should go: and when he is old, he will not depart from it" (KJV).

Deuteronomy 6:5-7 tells us to teach our children "diligently" (KJV) to love the Lord our God with all their heart, soul, and might—in the home, out of the home, in the morning, and at night. In short, all of the time.

The Word of God is clear about our obligation to teach our children in the way they "should" go. Our Christian belief in the Bible as truth demands that we make every effort to impress upon them the ideals of Christian ethics founded in God's Word.

The object of Christian schools is not to isolate our children from the practical knowledge necessary to function in the world today, but rather to provide them with basic Christian attitudes as a base for that knowledge. This will teach them how to use skills and learning to become a whole person according to the will of God. Christian schools are becoming more and more proficient in this method of instruction.

However, if children placed in Christian schools are to receive the educational training expected by public institutions of higher learning and the world in general, teaching at the primary and secondary levels must be up to par with that of public schools. Admittedly, not all Christian schools meet this level. But upon honest evaluation of public schools, can we say that all of them meet these standards? Many public schools fall far short of the scholastic ideals expected of Christian schools by their critics.

From a secular viewpoint, the schools that teach our children must instruct them in the fundamentals necessary to become responsible citizens in society. Requirements for the

My dad says you should be teaching us
how to get ahold of the apples in the first place.

acceptable proficiency in this task are expected to be established and enforced by governmental accreditation bodies. Given this basic level of training for fundamental education, our role as Christian parents becomes imperative. As Christians, we know there are other areas in which our children need training.

Gradually, throughout the history of public education, we have moved away from using methods and lesson materials that were strictly Bible-related text and application (as in McGuffey's Reader). We are now responding to the modern cry for more and more separation of church and state. No wonder the Christian schools in America have experienced such phenomenal growth in the past few years.

Where else could you find a balanced education coupled with the following aspects found in Christian schools:

1. Daily reinforcement of the parents' biblical responsibility to "Train up a child in the way he should go."

2. Reinforcement of the morals and religious convictions that are taught at home, giving support and credence to the disciplines of the family.

3. Centering Christ as the focal point in the study of each subject, so that a Christian perspective is achieved in the analytical process.

4. Confidence, as a parent, that the faculty and administration care about the spiritual side of human existence and that they model the Christian attitudes so important to the growing minds of our children.

With the introduction of electronic entertainment and the preoccupation of society with leisure time, the public schools of today have drastically changed lesson materials and methods to comply with secular demand. Sports and hobbies as well as other recreational activities are injected into the school curriculum with as much or more emphasis as the required fundamental subjects. These things are indeed important in Christian schools as well, to provide a balanced, well-rounded education. But in a Christian school, the primary emphasis is not placed on the external benefits of such activity. Rather, primary concern is placed on the internal well-being of the individual as it applies to the Christian life.

"And thou shalt love the Lord thy God with all thine heart, and with all thy soul, and with all thy might" (Deuteronomy 6:5, KJV). "And be not conformed to this world: but be ye transformed by the renewing of your mind, that ye may prove what is that good, and acceptable, and perfect, will of God" (Romans 12:2, KJV). Our children are human beings, with human needs and the desire to be a part of humanity. But achievement and fulfillment, both intellectually and socially, are not denied them in a Christian educational setting.

School districts are designated geographically so that there is little choice about where your child may attend public school. Christian schools, although not bound by districts and zones, are fewer in number and thus less accessible.

Even more constricting is the fact that not all Christian schools may be academically credible. But many are. And it is to those schools that we, as Christians, must pledge our support.

Even if the quality of public education is not decaying, contrary to what the media is reporting, then let us question the basis from which public education is taught. The Bible commissions us to teach our children diligently the commandments of God; it is our responsibility to do our best to achieve that goal.

Parents in increasing numbers are being **AGAINST** asked to support private Christian schools. After all, these are "Christian" schools, the argument goes. But the idea that they are religious, and therefore better, needs careful consideration.

In the early days of educational theory, people understood that the common school was a powerful force in developing the values of children. As a result, the doors were thrown wide open to Christian influence. The majority of evangelicals strongly supported the teaching of religion as a required subject.

Later, immigrants from the more liturgical churches arrived, and began sending their children to parochial schools. In this way their social ties were maintained and their culture preserved. A second reason for sending their children to parochial schools was in reaction to the emotional evangelical conversions. These schools were used to develop and train Christian character, in opposition to conversion.

Before the 1800s most public schools did not distinguish between secular and sacred. Catholic immigrants, however, multiplied the number of parochial schools. Fearing the Catholic impact on American culture, Protestant educational leaders decided to make the public schools sectarian. They hoped the deemphasis on religion would encourage Catholics to enroll students in the public school system.

This seems to have worked, since today the vast majority of school-age children attend public schools. These schools are microcosms of our society. As our values change, they are reflected in the schools. Problems in the culture become school problems. For example, stern discipline and traditional authority patterns have been rejected in schools, just as they have been in American homes.

In times of social crisis, parochial schools spring up, fueled by the fears of Christian parents. Today's proliferation of these schools is directly related to desegregation. Parents are withdrawing students from public schools to express frustration with and lack of control over influencing their children's attitudes. These parents reflect on the total control their own parents and grandparents had over them, and they long to have this same measure of control over their children. But they fail to see how this degree of control assured the passing down of parental prejudices.

Today some well-meaning parents expect children to grow into mirror images of themselves. Those who are successful in creating clones discover too late that their children do not adapt to the demands of a changing culture. They openly express a need to be insulated from a society over which they feel powerless. These Bible-believing folk retreat into a Christian subculture of their own design.

The current demand for parochial schools represents a complete reversal from that of early evangelicals. Over a period of time, attitudes crystallize along theological and denominational lines. Their immersion in the subculture leads them to lament their own impotence in perpetuating their faith in today's world.

Each of us must question whether the current popularity of parochial schools is evidence that we have lost faith in conversion as the instrument of spiritual change. Are we now joining forces with those liturgical brethren who believe that a child is educated into Christianity?

Long-term educational and spiritual goals are often sacrificed to short-term parochial school gains. Denominations that strongly advocate parochial schools experience a high incidence of loss to the church. As a result, these denominations are dropping in membership.

Further evidence indicates that one denomination that has been a traditionally strong supporter of Christian schools has closed one in every five schools in the last decade.

Private, Christian schools are not in a position to solve the major contemporary problems in society for the following reasons:

1. They rarely educate over 1% of American children in any community.
2. They are not representative of the population they serve.
3. Only a few impact education or society to any large degree.
4. Many exist for the wrong reasons.
5. They assume little responsibility for changing society.
6. Inflation makes it difficult to fund these schools adequately.
7. Low salaries make it difficult to recruit and retain qualified teachers.
8. Tuition costs prohibit attendance of students from lower income families.

Before agreeing to support parochial schools, Christians ought to consider some possible obstacles to their eventual success.

Many are locally controlled by their own goals and objectives. Therefore many operate without certification requirements. Private schools may not be held to public school standards of health, safety, or curriculum (lesson materials). Decisions concerning the length of school day and year are not mandated.

In some states parochial schools actively resist legislative regulations. Some have successfully argued that their entire allegiance is to God alone. Others have asked the courts to rule against certification and the monitoring of student enrollments.

These obstacles make it difficult for private, Christian schools to deal with the problems related to urban minorities, racial conflicts, the poor, or the handicapped. In order to make a difference in the years ahead, parochial schools need to immerse themselves in the social arena—educating and ministering across the culture.

If we Christians really believe that Christ is the source of all spiritual life, then let our faith and the faith of our children be tested in the marketplace of secular options—the public school.

## Reaction and Rebuttal

DR. EDWIN H. RAIN has some thoughts about Christian education that speak to an issue raised by Mr. Houser. In *Christianity and American Education,* page 236, Rain says, "Christian theory of education is an exposition of the idea that Christianity is a world and life view and not simply a series of unrelated doctrines. Christianity includes all of life. Every realm of knowledge, every aspect of life and every fact of the universe find their place and their answer within Christianity."

Christian education is not merely education by a Christian, it is education for a Christian. If we are to take the Bible seriously, with regard to educating our children, then we must teach each school subject—from mathematics to history—in the light of the Christian perspective.

FOR

21

Why, then, does Mr. Houser place on the Christian school the burden "to solve the major contemporary problems in society"? All the Christian school is trying to do is compare basic education to biblical truth. The "problems" and "obstacles" Mr. Houser speaks about are relevant only to the schools whose philosophy is not rooted in biblical theory. Schools that are philosophically and biblically sound deserve the support of all Christians. After all, the schools are striving to provide our children with quality education in the Christian tradition.

And by support I mean more than the mere payment of tuition to send a child to a Christian school. Support can be given only when the biblical ideals on which the institution is founded are either praised or constructively criticized for the sake of improvement.

THE DECISION to send a child to a Christian school should not be based on negative reactions **AGAINST** to the public school system. Separation of church and state is not a valid argument in favor of Christian education. Parents who surrender this long-established principle to their children's education are not serving the best interests of either.

Emphasis on sporting events and recreation has never been the primary focus of public schools, as evidenced by the number of students involved or the time allotted for these activities. Accreditation teams that pass judgment on schools continue to direct their attention to the minimal standards of activity necessary for the maintenance of good health.

Sending a child to a Christian school to accelerate learning is usually a poor investment. Figures reported by the U.S. Census Bureau indicate that private Christian schools educate only a small percent of selected students. They come from families whose income is 40% higher than those of students attending public schools. They are predominantly white, free of handicaps, and speak only one language. In spite of these factors, the most recent study comparing the growth of private and public school students found little or no difference in reading and math achievements.

When Christian schools graduate students with a greater application of scriptural knowledge, a higher level of personal and moral commitment, and higher academic achievement than their Christian public school peers, they will command our support.

Until then, private Christian education remains for the few a fond hope, and for most of us a worthy ideal.

*Shegay Vanderpool has taught for nine years in both public and Christian schools. She is married, has two children, and is presently living in La Crescenta, Calif.*

*Vern Houser is assistant superintendent of management and business in the Hueneme School District in Port Hueneme, Calif.*

## Chapter 3

*The Issue:*

# Capital Punishment

*Statement for Debate:*

**Capital punishment is necessary to protect innocent citizens and reduce crime.**

by

James Dean (For)

Clarence Bence (Against)

*Background Scripture:*

**Exodus 21:23-25; Matthew 5:38-44**

PRISON OFFICIALS in America have been releasing inmates at record numbers in recent ⎢ FOR ⎢ years, even though they realize over 80% of those inmates will commit another crime and return to prison.

Why do officials release the inmates? Overcrowding. It all stems from the growth of crime, and it represents our increased inability to protect our citizens against criminals.

Capital punishment is one method of protecting citizens against dangerous criminals. It is allowed in most states for only two principal reasons: (1) major assaults upon the person, such as murder, kidnapping, rape, bombing, and arson; and (2) major political crimes of espionage and treason. Former United States Attorney General Abe Fortas writes in *The Case Against Capital Punishment,* "The vast majority of capital offenses are murders committed in the course of armed robbery that result

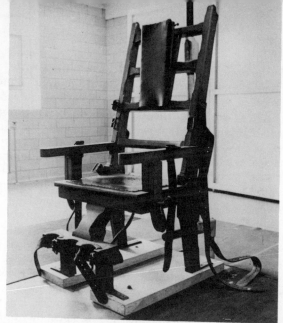

from fear, tension, or anger of the moment, and murders that are the result of passion or mental disorders."[1]

Authors Samuel Yochelson and Stanton Samenow, in a recently published, two-volume study called *The Criminal Personality,* argue, "The habitual criminal is a deceiver; he has little capacity for love, friendship, or companionship; he can commit brutal acts without a twinge of conscience and yet continue to believe he is a good person."[2] The criminal is chronically angry even as he walks down the street. Anger is a mental state that is sometimes expressed outwardly, but more often boils within. It is most dangerous when it is not on the surface. Anger is as basic to his personality as the iris is to the eye.[3]

Once a person has broken the law by venting his anger and deliberately killing another human, he can do so again and again with greater ease. Psychological studies bear this out.

When we look at the concept of protecting people against such criminals, we are really focusing on the concept of crime deterrence. The word *deter* is defined by Webster as "to discourage." Capital punishment is the most extreme form of deterrence.

In the book *Criminal Personality* the authors write "when a criminal commits a crime . . . he desires to avoid apprehension. We have used the phrase 'external deterrence' to label his fear of getting caught. At times conscience enters his stream of thinking and inhibits crime; we have labeled this the 'internal deterrent.'"[4] Now it appears we have two ways of looking at deterrence, one is externally, the other internally. External deterrents are: public opinion, police, courts, corrections including capital punishment. Internal deterrents include: strength of conscience, which cleansed by the power of the Holy Spirit will not permit us to violate laws of our society. Unfortunately, the further we violate that conscience, the more difficult it becomes to regain its proper use. The inner conscience, or internal deterrent, is by far the better of the two deterrents. However, when inner control fails, we have to use some form of outer control to protect those who abide by the law.

God has given to each of us the power of choice. This power of choice carries with it the awesome responsibility of facing the consequences of the choices made. But this is true only when we are made to consistently face up to those choices.

But are we consistent? The criminal justice system in its frantic effort to protect the defendant's rights, has become the main source of inconsistency. Little thought is given to the rights of the victim. Prison sentencing has become a laughing matter to the criminal. He knows that if he has money to pay for a good lawyer, he can avoid prison quite easily. Only 1 out of every 100 people arrested will ever receive a prison sentence. Those who are sentenced come to prison knowing they may be released in less than half the time given by the judge. The death penalty, too, has become a joke because a defendant can prolong the execution almost indefinitely with successive appeals.

In an ongoing study behind prison fences, I have been asking the question, "What keeps you from hitting the fence and escaping?" The prison I work at as staff psychologist is a 77-acre compound with double fences around it. These fences are erected on concrete walls. The fences are 10 feet high with a 2-foot Y arm on top, covered with barbed wire. There are six guard towers. The answer to my question is almost always, "Are you nuts? That's sure death. No way would I try that."

It seems to me the fence with its sure death symbol is a powerful deterrent to escape. Likewise, a consistent death penalty would be a powerful deterrent to crime. It might not deter the murder of passion nor the mentally ill. But to the cold, calculating murderer, it could have a powerful effect.

There is an old saying, "If the reward of crime exceeds the punishment of crime, crime will flourish." I believe if we elevate the punishment above the rewards, crime will diminish.

When we finally decide to get more consistent in the way we administer punishment and hold the individual responsible for his own behavior, then we will have taken a giant step toward reducing crime and protecting our citizens.

W<small>HEN WE HEAR</small> of a violent crime in which an innocent person has been killed, we often say **AGAINST** the criminal ought to pay for that crime with his life. This cry for retribution is a natural response of people who have been created in God's image and who share His concern for justice.

But does execution of a sinner serve any real purpose other than allowing society to express its disapproval of the crime and the criminal? I think not. And as a follower of Jesus Christ, I am called to a better, even though more costly, response to such sinful acts. My natural desire for justice must be tempered with a desire for mercy and for the redemption of those who have done wrong. Because I seek to express the message of Christ's forgiveness, I cannot call for the death of any person, no matter how undeserving of life that individual may be.

Many Christians do advocate capital punishment for serious crime; and they justify their position on the basis of sociological and biblical principles. But these reasons collapse under close examination. They ignore the revelation of Christ.

Many people argue that capital punishment is necessary to deter others from committing murder and serious crime. But no study has proven that execution of criminals deters crime. Most capital offenses are committed by people who act in a sudden moment of anger or passion, or else by a calculating individual who assumes he will never be caught. These criminals are not likely to be stopped by threats of the death penalty. Furthermore, if capital punishment would deter violent crime, then logic would suggest that executions should be public events covered extensively by the media so that their impact on society would be more effective. This is a policy few Christians would wish to endorse.

A second argument in favor of capital punishment is that execution is the only way to guarantee that some criminals do not repeat their horrible acts. But could not the problem be solved by other methods short of killing? Could there not be more effort given to rehabilitation? Or why not sentence the incorrigible to imprisonment without chance of parole? "Too costly," you reply. But dare we end anyone's life simply because the alternative is expensive? What nightmares do we introduce into our society when we use cost analysis to decide a person's right to live? In a free and moral society, we must be willing to take the risks and costs of protecting every human being's life. Christians who would defend the right to life for unborn infants, mentally retarded children, and terminally ill patients, dare not suggest that "bad people" should die simply because keeping them alive is a burden to society's pocketbook.

Beyond these sociological arguments, Christians look to the Bible for revelation of God's will on this matter. And some would point to the Old Testament where capital punishment was not only tolerated but also commanded by God. The standard passage that is quoted as favoring the death penalty is Exodus 21:23-25. It reads in part, "you shall appoint as a penalty life for life, eye for eye, tooth for tooth" (NASB). But the use of this passage raises several questions of interpretation. Old Testament scholars point out that instruction was not a call for severe treatment of criminals, but quite the opposite. In a culture where entire families or villages might be massacred in retaliation for some act, God *restricted* the punishment so it could not be greater than the crime committed. Only one life was to be taken for a murder, only a tooth could be demanded as payment for a lost tooth. How strange that we should take a passage meant to curb the human desire to "get even" and use it to justify a harsh view of justice today.

A second problem arises when we study this passage. Would those who advocate capital punishment want to interpret this whole passage literally and demand a one-for-one payment for all types of physical abuse? Would they torture the torturer, mutilate the mutilator, shoot the armed assailant in the same way he had wounded his victim? Is it not more sensible to view this passage as God's partial revelation to an underdeveloped and unchristian society that has now been replaced by a higher standard of justice and grace in the New Covenant?

Jesus quoted this very passage when He was declaring that He was calling His followers to a new law. In Matthew 5:38-44 He supersedes the older system of justice with new instructions to "not resist him who is evil," but rather to "love your enemies." In Romans 12:19 we are told to overcome the natural desire for retribution and to do good to our enemies. These scriptures may seem unrealistic in today's world, but there is no exemption clause in the Bible that allows us to treat criminals differently than Christ commands. In fact, it is precisely those whom we find most difficult to love who demand the greatest demonstration of mercy and grace. Love requires us to extend forgiveness and the possibility for spiritual transformation to even these who seem so far from the kingdom of God.

"But they don't deserve to live." This final argument for capital punishment sounds so hollow when spoken by a Christian. In God's eyes, we all had forfeited our rights to eternal life. Yet He saw in us possibilities of redemption. Rather than demanding the spiritual death penalty from us, He paid a great price so that we might be rehabilitated.

How can we who have been freed from the prison of sin, and who pray, "forgive us our sins, just as we forgive others" treat fellow humans with less compassion and mercy?

## Reaction and Rebuttal

**M**Y OPPONENT SAYS that capital punishment does not deter crime. But no study can accurately | FOR |

29

measure the number of times a crime isn't committed. So we have no way of measuring the number of people who aren't killed each year because of the fear of capital punishment.

Mr. Bence argues the need for more rehabilitative services. The old saying, "You can lead a horse to water, but you can't make him drink," applies here. Rehabilitation services are usually provided in the modern prison of today. However, the responsibility of being rehabilitated is the inmate's. No one can force him to learn or change.

Frequently, vocational education aimed at rehabilitation serves only to sharpen the skills used in crime. Welding class teaches him how to open a safe. Electrical wiring class is a great place to learn how to deactivate an alarm system. Only the inmate can rehabilitate himself—but he is usually more intent on pursuing his criminal life. This is confirmed by the number of criminals who return to prison after being released.

So, how should we respond to the question, how can I—a member of the Christian society—call for the death of someone who has committed a crime? When will we learn that society isn't responsible for all of a person's choices? In John 10:18, Jesus said, "No one takes it [my life] from me, but I lay it down of my own accord."

I believe in the power of choice and in my freedom to choose the path I follow in life. The criminal chooses his own path. Society doesn't force him into it. It is a way of life. When a person takes another person's life in a malicious manner, he should know he will forfeit his own right to live.

Mr. Dean uses statistics and sociological **AGAINST** studies to support his views. But where are the biblical arguments? As Christians, we are interested in the opinions and research of others; but we must finally decide what is right and wrong on the basis of biblical principles God reveals to us in His Word. Attorney generals and secular scientists may be wrong concerning moral judgments. I want biblical reasons before I am willing to take another life.

My opponent uses two basic arguments to defend the execution of criminals: the overcrowding of our prisons, and the deterrence of would-be criminals. The first is really an economic problem, and I have already spoken about the dangers of making moral judgments based on financial considerations.

Whether capital punishment deters crime is still a debatable question. But for the sake of argument, let's suppose that it does. Striking a child with a stick might deter him from sucking his thumb, but we cannot justify child abuse on the grounds that it prevents bad manners. How much more should we question the argument that killing people is morally right because it prevents bad actions in others! Certainly we would want to do what we could to prevent crime in our society. But the ends do not justify the means, when the means used are morally wrong.

The execution of a person is the deliberate termination of a God-given life. Rather than execute criminals, I would prefer to speak out boldly against sin and crime, do what I can to restrain wicked people from repeating their acts, while working to rehabilitate them spiritually and socially into the human beings God intended them to be.

1. Abe Fortas, *The Case Against Capital Punishment* (Duskin Publication, Annual Edition 80/81), 203.

2. Samuel Yochelson and Stanton E. Samenow, *The Criminal Personality* (New York: Jason Armson of New York, 1976), 1:268.

3. Michael S. Sevrill, *A Cold New Look at the Criminal Mind* (Duskin Publication, Annual Edition 80/81), 44.

4. Yochelson and Samenow, *The Criminal Personality*, 2:327.

*James Dean is chief of psychological services at a maximum security youth prison in Florida.*

*Clarence Bence is associate professor of pastoral ministries and church history at Marion College, Marion, Ind.*

## Chapter 4

*The Issue:*

# War

*Statement for Debate:*

**Christians are obligated to support their country at war, including military service if needed.**

by

Earl C. Wolf (For)

Richard H. Leffel (Against)

*Background Scripture:*

**Acts 5:27-32; Romans 13:1-7**

CHRISTIANS share the hope of the young prophet Isaiah who foresaw a day when war | FOR | would end. He believed that day would come when God

> *will judge between the nations*
> *and will settle disputes for many peoples.*
> *They will beat their swords into plowshares*
> *and their spears into pruning hooks.*
> *Nation will not take up sword against nation,*
> *nor will they train for war anymore* (Isaiah 2:4).

But that day has not yet come. And until it does, Christians must live as citizens of two worlds. We are members of the community of faith, but we are also citizens of the state. If we emphasize only our loyalty to the kingdom of God, we will fail in our responsibility to an earthly kingdom of mankind. And on the other hand, if we live only for the state, we will miss that everlasting Kingdom.

Sometimes these two kingdoms come into conflict. There are times when, as Christians, we must declare it our duty to obey God rather than men. But that is the exception to the rule. Normally Christians accept and support their civil government.

Tension between these two kingdoms has always been a part of the Christian's life. Jesus focused on dual loyalties when He said, "Give to Caesar what is Caesar's, and to God what is God's" (Matthew 22:21). This was not just a clever response to His enemies, it was a declaration of principle: submission to an earthly government. He lived out this principle by paying His taxes and teaching His disciples to do the same (Matthew 17:27).

Is the matter of going to war one of those times when a Christian must obey God rather than men?

Men have debated this for centuries. Some feel that non-resistance is the only position for the Christian—that we can participate in war only as noncombatants. The pacifist says the Christian must have nothing to do with war. Others believe Christians can participate only in defensive warfare. Finally, some Christians believe they are obligated to engage in war to stop attack or to correct cruel injustices to mankind.

The proponents of nonresistance and pacifism often call attention to the sixth commandment, "You shall not murder" (Exodus 20:13), which deals with hatred and intent to murder (Matthew 19:18). Of itself, however, the sixth commandment does not help us sort out the answer to the complex issue of war. Under the Mosaic law, capital punishment was permitted for a number of crimes. Furthermore, under the Old Covenant killing in self-defense was not considered a criminal act.

As the Christian deals with the complex issues of war, he must consider other Bible passages. Romans 13:1-7 is most important. Writing to Christians who lived within sight of Caesar's palace, Paul stressed that government is ordained of God. Therefore, it is a serious matter to fail in our responsibilities to civil government and to go off doing as we see fit (Judges 21:25).

The apostle Peter joins Paul in emphasizing obedience to government. While Christians are "aliens and strangers in the world," they are still supposed to submit to governmental authority (1 Peter 2:11-25). With a tyrant such as Nero on the throne at the time of Peter's writing, Christians were still urged to honor him and submit to his authority. In our day, too, we are to share in God's purpose of order in human society.

The collective judgment of my own denomination has something to say on the subject of war and military service:

We believe that the ideal world condition is that of peace and that it is the full obligation of the Christian Church to use its influence to seek such means as will enable the nations of earth to be at peace and to devote all of its energies for the propagation of the message of peace.

However, we realize that we are living in a world where evil forces and philosophies are actively in conflict with these Christian ideals and that there may arise such international emergencies as will require a nation to resort to war in defense of its ideals, its freedom, and its existence.[1]

This statement continues and allows for those "who have conscientious objections to certain forms of military service." But it also clearly states that my denomination is not one of the "recognized noncombatant religious organizations."

Several years ago I attended a military personnel retreat at Berchtesgaden, West Germany. Assembled were military chaplains and over 200 enlisted men and their families. On this trip I visited Hitler's *Kehlsteinhaus,* or "Tea-House," perched on a mountain peak overlooking Salzburg, Austria. This "Tea-House" on Eagle's Nest was built for Hitler's personal enjoyment at an enormous cost to the Nazi party and the German people.

Following the retreat we visited Dachau concentration camp near Munich. This camp was set up by the Nazi SS in 1933. More than 200,000 prisoners were registered here between 1933 and 1945. Nearly 32,000 deaths can be certified, besides the thousands killed before registration. I will never forget the film I saw there that showed trainloads of people headed for the gas furnaces.

This unforgettable experience prompts some questions.

If Hitler's international aggression could have been stopped earlier, how many Jews would have been saved? Would a stance of nonresistance have stopped Hitler's mad rush to conquer the world? Should Hitler have been permitted to continue his atrocious acts against humanity and kill the Jewish people in nation after nation? Would pacifism have stopped the killing? Would love have halted Hitler? If the 6 million Jews that Hitler had killed could speak today, what would they say to us?

Living as citizens of two worlds is an awesome responsibility.

Writer Myron S. Augsburger once **AGAINST** penned this observation, "God has disarmed the Christian . . . Having been disarmed by God, we lay aside guns and bombs because they are too weak to achieve his goals." Then he poses the unsettling question, "If God has disarmed the Christian, on whose authority does a Christian pick up arms again?"[2]

Christians should not be obligated to support their country at war.

### The Biblical Argument

*The Old Testament teachings call for peace.* In spite of some battles fought and won by God's people, the Old Testament reveals Jehovah's intent for His people: peace *(shalom)*.

*The New Testament message of Christ and the apostles is emphasized.* Jesus taught and practiced unconditional forgiveness and the love of enemies. And His death upon the Cross was a final rejection of violence and power.

All of Jesus' teachings, including the Sermon on the Mount, opposed all public evils—racial discrimination, cruelty, oppression, hypocrisy, deceit, corruption, and war—especially war. Writer Robert McAfee Brown notes, "Nothing in Jesus' life or teachings can be 'twisted' in support of killing or warfare."[3]

*Christ's gospel and the New Testament writers call for rec-*

*onciliation of a national enemy; not destruction.* The New Testament calls the Christian to work for redemption as opposed to annihilation.

Bible student Robert C. Detweiler says, "To preach a gospel of reconciliation while at the same time supporting or even participating in military action as the will of God is the height of contradiction."[4]

Participation in war, with its consequent slaughter of God-created human beings, is biblically unsupportable.

## The Historical Argument

*The example of Christ and the apostles was that they always refused to fight.* The French writer, Jean Lasserre, declares: "Neither Christ or his apostles ever recommended lethal violence."[5] Christ and His disciples always refused to fight, except for Peter's sword-wielding in Gethsemane, for which he was soundly rebuked by our Lord (see Matthew 26:51-54; Luke 22:49-51; John 18:10-11).

*The Early Church firmly and emphatically refused participation in war.* Modern church historians are agreed that war was condemned in the church for nearly three centuries, until Constantine officialized the Christian faith in A.D. 313.

Writer Ronald J. Sider asks, "Might there be more hope in the road walked by the Christians of the first three centuries? Might they perhaps have understood the mind of Christ more closely than subsequent generations?"[6]

*The "just war" theory has never worked in past history, and cannot succeed in a modern nuclear society.* Saint Augustine promoted the "just war" theory in the fourth century, and with it the church opened the door to military participation by Christians. This theory contended that under strictly adhered to conditions, a particular war might be permissible for Christians to engage in.

The "just war" theory, in history, has never worked and remains only a theory. And modern nuclear war capabilities now render the theory completely useless.

# The Moral Argument

*Man's conscience must follow the higher law of God, above loyalty to government.* Ultimately the "morality" of military participation by Christians must be answered by individual conscience.

Ronald J. Sider states, "Unless we deny our Lord, our loyalty to Christ's worldwide body of brothers and sisters must far exceed any loyalty to nation or country."[7]

The New Testament imposes limitations on governmental authority. All citizens are to honor the state, not seek to overthrow, and obey as long as its mandates are not in conflict with God's will (see 1 Timothy 2:1-2; Acts 5:29). But governmental authority is always subservient to God's law.

*War always involves sin and the killing of mankind, and must be repudiated by the Christian.* Since sin is the root of war, it follows that in combat the contradiction of one believer killing another believer—or unbeliever—both for whom Christ died, comes into conflict. John M. Drescher alludes to this dilemma: "Each person I face in combat is either a Christian or a non-Christian. If I destroy a Christian, I kill the brother for whom Scripture says I should lay down my life. If my enemy is a non-Christian, I destroy one for whom Christ died and take away any further opportunity to be a reconciler or to let him find salvation. In the interest of the gospel and salvation, I cannot participate in war."[8]

*Participation in modern nuclear warfare is to share the blame of the destruction of mankind.* Former American President Jimmy Carter said, "In an all-out nuclear war, more destructive power than in all of World War II would be unleashed every second for the long afternoon it would take for all the missiles and bombs to fall. A World War II every second—more people killed in the first few hours than all the wars of history put together."[9]

Today's Christian must soberly rethink his commitment. Is it toward Christ's principle of global evangelism, or is it toward modern man's insistence on world suicide? Will we follow the Bomb or the Cross? As Bible student Jim Wallis writes,

"The sign of the nuclear age is the Bomb. The sign of Christ is the Cross. The Bomb is the countersign to the Cross; it arrogantly threatens to undo the work that the Cross has done. . . . Which will hold sway in our times?"[10]

In the age of nuclear weapons, when the destruction of the world is a push of a button away, the church needs to reject war absolutely. Christ's followers should place all their energies into efforts of reconciliation, instead of human annihilation.

## Reaction and Rebuttal

IN HIS VIEW of nonresistance and pacifism, my opponent calls attention to the self-giving love

**FOR**

of Jesus—and rightly so. But he overlooks the fact that there is also "the wrath of the Lamb" (Revelation 6:16). There is both "the goodness and severity of God" (Romans 11:22, KJV).

During a Jewish Passover, Jesus discovered the profaning of the Temple. "So he made a whip out of cords, and drove all from the temple area . . . he scattered the coins of the money changers and overturned their tables. To those who sold doves he said, 'Get these out of here! How dare you turn my Father's house into a market!'" (John 2:15-16). Jesus was outraged at the desecration of the Temple.

As Christians, are we not to be outraged by abominable crimes against the human race?

Pacifism emphasizes the dignity of human life, but rejects the need for governments to use force to save innocent and defenseless people against aggressive inhumanities. Is not stopping a mad killer a real way to show respect to intended victims by preserving their lives?

Ours is a sinful, complex world. It is not a utopian society. That is why God saw the need for government, and ordained it. God considers order better than chaos. That's why He urges us to support government. We enjoy its benefits. We go to the ballot box, and we pay our taxes. Are we not to support our government also when it must use force to stop attack or correct horrifying injustices?

MAJOR ARGUMENTS supporting a Christian's AGAINST
participation in war usually include:

- Obedience to civil government
- Conformity to church standards
- Deterrent to unavoidable world evil

But our Christian conscience must sometimes overrule the state.

For example, are Christians to accept abortion as morally right because a government legalizes it?

Is a Christian bound to support homosexuality because civil law upholds that behavior?

Are we to approve of gambling in the form of legalized lottery because our state now allows it?

Certainly not! The conscientious Christian must respond with a resounding "NO" to such flagrant violations of the Christian ethic. And so it is in war, involving the slaughter of souls for whom Christ died. Here a Christian must first answer to his own individual conscience, which has been molded by God. Let us stand for right on this issue—and if need be, oppose civil authority—as we do in other matters of Christian conscience.

Some denominational statements allow Christians to participate in war. But it takes far more than that to make such participation acceptable before God. Let every Christian make the Bible, with the loving teachings and noncombatant example of Jesus, the manual to guide his behavior.

War, hatred, and injustice are ever with us in this world. But that in no way sanctions a Christian's support of war.

Tertullian wrote in the third century, "How can we wage war without the sword that God has taken away from us? How can we learn the use of the sword, when our Lord said that he who raised the sword would perish by the sword? And how can the sons of peace take part in combat?"

The Christian's only sword is the Word of God. With it we will win souls and not take lives, instruct and not injure, bring life instead of death.

1. *Manual* (Kansas City: Nazarene Publishing House, 1980), 340-41.

2. John M. Drescher, *Why I Am a Conscientious Objector* (Scottsdale: Herald Press, 1983), 11.

3. Ibid., 33.

4. Richard C. Detweiler, *Mennonite Statements on Peace* (Scottsdale: Herald Press, 1968).

5. Jean Lasserre, *War and the Gospel* (Scottsdale: Herald Press, 1974), 53.

6. Ronald J. Sider and Richard K. Taylor, *Nuclear Holocaust & Christian Hope* (Downers Grove, Ill.: InterVarsity Press, 1982), 92.

7. Ibid., 84.

8. Drescher, *Conscientious Objector,* 38-39.

9. Jimmy Carter, Farewell Speech, January 14, 1981.

10. Jim Wallis, *Call to Conversion* (New York: Harper & Row, 1981), 88.

*Earl C. Wolf*
*is a retired editor and director of*
*Chaplaincy Services for the Church*
*of the Nazarene, Kansas City.*

*Richard H. Leffel*
*is a pastor in Amarillo, Tex.*

## Chapter 5

*The Issue:*

# Lowering Our Standard of Living

---

*Statement for Debate:*

**Christians must lower their standard of living and give the extra money to help alleviate human need.**

by

Jon Johnston (For)

Byron C. Ford (Against)

---

*Background Scripture:*

**Isaiah 3:10; Luke 12:13-21; 2 Thessalonians 3:6-13**

---

**T**. S. ELIOT'S PREDICTION may not be too far off. Someday America's gravestone could read: | FOR | "Here lies a decent, godless people. Their only monument to civilization was an asphalt road and one thousand lost golf balls."[1]

Materialism saturates every facet of American life. It pulls so strongly that it might be considered an "undertow." Certainly, essential values like self-sacrifice and human dignity are being submerged.

The message is loud and clear: Acquire more. Acquire the best. And don't hesitate. Rush to surround yourself with the very latest and most technologically advanced gadgets. Then,

"I don't recommend the quiche—the dog's been in it."

flaunt them in a society that largely judges human worth by such trinkets and toys.

If you aren't successful in this bewildering game, fake it. Pretend. What you cannot afford, buy on credit. Sew designer labels in inferior clothing. Put a bumper sticker on your old clunker that reads: "My other car is a Mercedes."

This nation's materialistic undertow is no respecter of persons. It inundates not only the wealthy who buy at Nieman Marcus—but also the struggling poor who wishfully gaze at products advertised on TV. It pulls under the wicked who acquire by unethical means—but also submerges far too many evangelical Christians *who should know better.*

Evangelical scholar Carl F. H. Henry does not mince words in declaring:

> American evangelicalism is being spiritually thwarted by its affluence. No group of Christians has ... more to learn about sacrifice ... [our] lifestyles are clearly nonchristian ... marked by greed, extravagance,

self-gratification, [and] lack of compassion for the needy.[2]

The twice-born who indulge in (or set their affections on) a materialistic life-style are quick to defend themselves:

"My wealth convinces impoverished non-Christians that God takes good care of His followers." (It also could convince them of your selfishness.)

"Why refuse the material blessings that God pours upon me?" (Whether to refuse such gifts is not the crucial issue. Rather, it is the necessity of sharing your bounty.)

My position is very simple: Those of us who claim to follow the "lowly One of Galilee" must disentangle ourselves from the materialistic net. Priorities must be reestablished, so that our lives exude simplicity and moderation. So that our fulfillment is based on our vibrant relationship with Him—rather than on things. For many of us, this will mean a scaling-down of our life-styles and a modification of our life's ambitions.

What benefits result from following the pattern of simplicity? There are many. Among them:

**1. Avoidance of Danger.** "Then he said to them, 'Watch out! Be on your guard against all kinds of *greed;* a man's life does not consist in the abundance of his possessions'" (Luke 12:15).

**2. Cultivation of Inner Contentment.** "Keep your lives free from the love of money and be content with what you have, because God has said, 'Never will I leave you; never will I forsake you'" (Hebrews 13:5).

**3. Possession of True Security.** "Command those who are rich in this present world not to . . . put their hope in wealth, which is so uncertain, but to put their hope in God . . . In this way they will lay up treasure for themselves as a firm foundation for the coming age, so that they may take hold of the life that is truly life" (1 Timothy 6:17, 19).

Jesus, our supreme Example, had a loose attachment to things. He lovingly relinquished heaven's privileges in order to endure earth's rejection. Unlike the foxes and birds, He owned no home. Though sorely tempted at a time of great physical exhaustion, He emphatically rejected Satan's offer of bread, king-doms, and fame. It is true that He never lauded poverty, nor debased His Heavenly Father's material universe. Nevertheless, our Lord chose simplicity.

As a result, His life was free from worldly entanglements. And He was free to obey God. Lacking luxuries that would separate Him from the desperate persons He desired to serve, He was approachable to all manner of men. The point is clear. Our Savior renounced a materialistic life-style in order to give more to those in need.

Likewise, the purpose of denying ourselves is to be able to give more in His name. Then, we are better prepared to follow His instruction in the Parable of the Good Samaritan—to truly be a loving and generous servant to our brother in need.

Ten thousand in our world die each day. More than 1 bil-lion of our brothers and sisters are severely malnourished and waste away. And here is the saddest fact of all: there is enough food to go around—if the planet's affluent would only share.

With these facts in mind, how can today's conscientious Christian fail to reduce his standard of living, climb off the materialistic treadmill, and channel his resources to those in need? It's really not optional. The obedient, heaven-bound Christian will share. Jesus stated it plainly, "From everyone who has been given much, much will be demanded; and from the one who has been entrusted with much, much more will be asked" (Luke 12:48b).

In short, God expects us to: (1) reduce our standard of living to a level of simplicity and moderation; and, (2) give of our surplus to those who are in need—and for whom Jesus died. If we will abide by this biblical admonition, our desperate world will be revolutionized, our Church will experience renewal, and we will have that blessed inner assurance that results from obedience.

My friend and popular speaker-author, Tony Campolo, tells about his visit to Haiti. His gracious hosts ushered him to a beautiful restaurant, where he was served a delicious meal. But as he ate, he happened to look outside. There they were. Eight hungry Haitian children, with their noses pressed up against the glass. All staring at Tony's thick steak. He immediately lost his appetite and dropped his fork. The waiter, seeing what was happening, quickly moved to pull down the blind. He said to Tony, "Enjoy your meal. Don't let them bother you."[3]

May God help us to never pull down the blind.


EUROPEAN SOCIETY in the Middle Ages operated on this premise: to him that has shall more **AGAINST** be given, and from him that has not shall be taken. Thus the feudal masters of the aristocracy exploited the majority who were serfs.

French guilds, on the other hand, insisted that every brother share his good fortune with another in an attempt to check what they called "economic egotism."

Much of today's society believes it is not that wealth should be distributed but that there should be greater wealth through more opportunity for all. Each person has been encouraged to contribute his creative ability to a burgeoning economy, with the idea that efficient use of wealth will insure prosperity. In such a system as this no one can long give something for nothing. Adequate production can come only if everyone shares in its work and results.

It is impractical to expect that a Christian should lower his standard of living and give the extra money to the poor. A man cannot rightly balance life and at the same time delve out most of his money to alleviate human need. It is his dignity that helps a man continue to earn wages. If he ceased to respectably support himself, the poor could be helped only temporarily at best. The mutuality of a give-and-take attitude allows for both sides to keep their dignity—the prosperous and the not so prosperous, the rich and poor.

Isaiah 3:10 records, "Say ye to the righteous, that it shall be well with him: for they shall eat the fruit of their doings" (KJV). The "something for nothing" policy will not produce utopia nor will it finally keep all the poor from starvation. People must have values. Something for something!

John Calvin condemned indiscriminate almsgiving. He encouraged the clergy to visit families and see if any were idle or drunken. St. Paul was quoted as the foundation for this rule, for he had written, "If a man will not work, he shall not eat" (2 Thessalonians 3:10).

The treasuries of many charitable agencies should simply not have access to the Christian's dollar. The Christian should also have personal control of his dollar. If this does not exist, a man cannot long be productive. He will be like the man William Graham Sumner (1840-1910) spoke of in his defense for our economic system. Sumner, once an Episcopal priest, turned to teaching at Yale as an economics professor. He made the statement that A and B got together to decide what C should do for D. In bearing the burden, C became the forgotten man.

The idea of one lowering his standard of living and giving the extra money to the poor smacks of a socialistic/communistic philosophy. This give-away doctrine will end in a dictatorial atheism.

Paternalism is not workable. The poor are not to be patronized by handouts. They should be given a chance for useful creativeness. The Roosevelt administration during the Great Depression realized that giving out food packages was not the answer to unemployment. The pride of people was at stake. Recipients would often be personally offended, their initiative thwarted. Relief needed to be doled out through wages for work projects, something for something! As a result of the discovery, the WPA (Work Progress Administration) was formed.

The redistribution of a man's wealth to the poor would have an adverse effect upon society in general. A sudden withdrawal of capital investment from some meaningful enterprise could cause more harm than good. If the few do not succeed, then not only the minority but also the majority will fall.

Any society, to a certain degree, practices the redistribution of wealth. Governments are doing this with our money all the time. Our present base of taxes support welfare and social security, along with local, state, and federal agencies. Enough is enough of something for nothing.

There is another practical reason that abolition of poverty cannot come from the redistribution of another's wealth. Taking from the "better-off" and giving to the poorer will not rectify their state if their philosophy of life stays the same.

A culture that has hard work, thrift, productivity, and frugality as its basis will develop economically to satisfaction. Among the many good results of the Reformation has been the Protestant liberty of creativeness and right to possess personal property for development. Innovation on the road to economic success has been paved by this newfound liberty.

To ease human suffering is noble work. But put yourself in the well-to-do man's shoes. He has labored energetically to earn his possessions. Will he want to earn more if it is taken from him? Why not let his money be put to use through his own creativeness? This, in turn, will give to the poorer opportunity for personal support.

## Reaction and Rebuttal

I WISH TO CHALLENGE some of my colleague's statements. Granted, we do live in a land of [FOR] equality. But as Abe Lincoln once put it: "Some are more equal than others."

It seems obvious that certain categories of people have been discriminated against. Because of this, some find it much easier to succeed. Others try hard for a while, but finally become dispirited and give up.

We must find some way to help those who are desperate. As followers of the lowly Man of Galilee, we must not flaunt our affluence. Instead, we need to live simply and share with the needy. Such sacrificial generosity can only add to the dignity of both giver and receiver. This does not mean, as my counterpart seems to imply, that the Christian will neglect his own basic needs. Nor will he seek to cultivate a paternalistic dependence on the part of the recipient.

Granted, some Old Testament verses seem to suggest that the righteous will prosper. However, much is said about sharing material bounty with the poor. The poor, for example, could legally take grain from farmers' fields and systematically had debts canceled during the Year of Jubilee. Ancient Hebrew society sought to redistribute wealth, and Old Testament prophets continually commanded the rich to share.

My colleague states that Calvin warned against indiscriminate almsgiving. Calvin was right. The Christian donor must seek God's guidance in fulfilling specific commitments of stewardship. However, the fact that there are unworthy recipients does not negate the necessity of sharing. And He has a way of revealing just who needs our help.

Finally, for Christians to scale down exorbitant tastes, and to share with the needy will not destroy capitalism. Instead, after seeing that others truly care, and that the world does not have to be a jungle, the weak among us will respond with rejuvenated motivation.

Like it or not, we are our brother's keeper. Accepting this fact can only create a better society.

$D$R. JOHNSTON'S ARGUMENT contains three major points: **AGAINST**

1. Materialism has caught evangelical Christians off guard;

2. Having plenty limits spirituality;

3. Right priorities place God before things.

His conclusion calls for a remedy that includes scaling down, modifying, and simplifying life—steps, he suggests, that help us avoid many problems and make it easier for us to supply the needs of the poor.

Dr. Johnston has built a "straw man" and has given him a thrashing.

The demanded remedy does not recognize that we have the poor with us—always. There is no simplistic cure. Besides, God requires 100%, doesn't He? Elijah requested the widow's last meal. Can there be an attitude of surplus giving that holds back even the necessities?

The proposal violates the scriptural truth of judging "someone else's servant" (Romans 14:4). We are responsible only to our own Master. How a Christian handles his finances is such a sensitive area that only the Lord can judge right from wrong. Materialistic tares are separated from the wheat by the Lord. So, Dr. Johnston's measuring stick ignores Christ's Lordship.

In fact, he actually has the branches pruning themselves. Yet Jesus said, "I am the vine; you are the branches ... my Father is the gardener" (John 15:5, 1). We are to abide in Him. God will prune the unfruitful branches.

The Church has benefited from capitalism. Because we have enjoyed above-average paychecks, tens of thousands have been able to go abroad as missionaries to spread the Good News. It is as though God has made us a global treasury to finance hundreds of clinics, hospitals, and schools around the globe.

The kingdom of heaven has been expanded through the giving attitude of prosperous, capitalistic Christians! It is only in recent years, as our generosity has lost its spiritual moorings, that giving has been supplanted by folly and selfishness.

1. Jess Moody, *A Drink at Joel's Place* (Waco, Tex.: Word, 1967), 41-42.

2. Carl F. H. Henry, "Evangelicals: Out of the Closet but Going Nowhere," *Christianity Today* 4 (January 1980) : 21.

3. Anthony Campolo, Jr., *The Success Fantasy* (Wheaton, Ill.: Victor Books, 1980), 144.

*Jon Johnston is professor of sociology and anthropology at Pepperdine University, Malibu, Calif.*

*Byron C. Ford is a pastor in Fairfield, Calif.*

## Chapter 6

*The Issue:*

# Supporting Israel

---

*Statement for Debate:*

**Because of biblical promises, Christians have an obligation to insure the future well-being of Israel.**

by

C. D. Hansen (For)

Ivan A. Beals (Against)

---

*Background Scripture:*

**Genesis 12:1-3; 15:18-21; 18:18-19**

---

PERHAPS NO SURVIVING PEOPLE have been more misunderstood, maligned, persecuted, | FOR | slaughtered, and scattered through the centuries than have the Jews. So vicious have been the attacks and persecution upon them that millions have been exterminated.

Much of the opposition Jews have faced, though, has been because of their continual disobedience to God. And since their return to Palestine and their restoration as a nation, Israel has been the constant focus of world attention and criticism. One has only to casually read the newspaper or listen to news broadcasts to understand the burden the world community has about what to do with this bitter cup described in Zechariah 12:1-3.

Why, then, should Israel be so important to Christians and what should be our motive for wanting to preserve her as a nation?

There are many reasons: humanitarian, historical, legal, and most importantly, theological. The theological reason is founded on God's covenant with Abraham as stated in Genesis 12:1-3; 15:18; and 18:18.

Let's review the four promises God made to Abraham in His covenant.

First, God promised that Abraham and his descendants would be given all the land "from the river of Egypt to the great river, the River Euphrates" (Genesis 15:18, NKJV). (The Euphrates is north of Palestine and would be the northern boundary. And the Nile in Egypt would be the southern boundary.) All this land would include most of Syria and all of Lebanon. And that that possession would be forever (Genesis 17:8).

From A.D. 70 when Titus and his Roman legions sacked and destroyed Jerusalem until May 14, 1948, the Jews had been dispersed across the globe and their land occupied by the Romans, Moslems, Turks, and Arabs.

After World War II the final plans of God's covenant with Abraham began to unfold as Jews forced their way into Palestine after almost 2,000 years of wanderings, and Israel became an independent and sovereign state officially recognized by the United Nations. Israel now had her own government, flag, and military power. Thus the prophecy of Jeremiah 32:37, 43-44, was fulfilled.

Most people can understand the bitter opposition of surrounding nations as they watched a wasteland they had occupied blossom into a rose as swamps were drained, trees were planted, and buildings, roads, and cities were built. And so, the prophecy of Ezekiel 36:5-11 came to pass.

For the Christian, the restoration of Israel as a nation is crucial. This is because many biblical scholars view Israel as God's prophetic timepiece pointing to the Second Coming, as suggested by the budding of the fig tree in Matthew 24.

Second, God promised that through Abraham Israel would become a great and righteous nation. He would be favored in such a way that the whole earth would benefit. How would this happen?

The Bible vividly portrays Israel as the object of God's blessing, kindness, and interest.

For example, David declared, "For the Lord has chosen Jacob for Himself, Israel for His special treasure" (Psalm 135:4, NKJV).

Moses recorded, "For the Lord's portion is His people; Jacob is the place of His inheritance. He found him in a desert land and in the wasteland, a howling wilderness; He encircled him, He instructed him, He kept him as the apple of His eye" (Deuteronomy 32:9-10, NKJV).

Paul reveals that through Israel would come the message of salvation. It was Israel that was first granted the special privileges of "the adoption, the glory, the covenants, the giving of the law, the service of God, and the promises" (Romans 9:4, NKJV).

As someone has succinctly stated, "Chosen by God, Israel was destined to make mankind aware of His sovereignty and grace. By her laws, she would witness to the Lord's holiness and justice. Her eternal truths would be revealed and recorded through her. And best of all, through the line of Abraham, the promised Messiah would enter the world" (compare Romans 9:5; 11:25-27).[1]

Third, God declared that He would punish and curse those nations that choose to act against His covenant with Abraham (Genesis 12:3).

Zechariah emphatically states, "For he who touches you [Israel] touches the apple of His eye" (Zechariah 2:8, NKJV).

Perhaps author Charles C. Ryrie summarizes the impact of this declaration best in his book *The Basis of the Premillennial Faith*. "History has borne out the fact that nations which have persecuted Israel, even when that very persecution was in fulfillment of God's discipline, have been punished for dealing with Abraham's seed."[2]

So, if for no other reason than a selfish one, Christian nations should take special care not to act against Israel.

Fourth, God promised that He would bless those who blessed Israel.

In other words, the nation that honors Israel will be honored by God. Therefore, government leaders should act wisely and prudently within God's perfect will in dealing with God's chosen people.

Finally, Christians should love the Jewish people and take an interest in them because they have a unique place in God's program. Jesus was a Jew, and through the Jews came the Holy Scriptures, the revelation of God to man, and the message of salvation.

Although many Jews have returned to their Hebrew language, customs, and homeland, Israel has not returned to God nor accepted Jesus as the Messiah. For the most part they believe that what they have accomplished through restoration of their land and suppressing foreign aggressors has been on their own power rather than on divine direction.

But God is not finished with His people yet—there is more to come. And as Christians we must stand with Israel or die as a nation and as a people.

**D**URING ISRAEL'S DRIVE to oust the PLO from Lebanon, jolting news came out of Beirut. **AGAINST** The headlines read, "600 Palestinians Massacred." Those killed were not known members of the Palestine Liberation Organization. They were unarmed men, women, and children in the Sabra and Chatilla refugee camps, slain by Lebanese militiamen. But the area was lighted by Israeli flares and controlled by Israel's army.

Investigations failed to prove actual participation by Israel's military. Eventually, though, the finger of guilt and responsibility forced the resignation of Israeli Defense Minister Ariel Sharon. Such acts have caused some Christians to question the extent to which they should support Israel in her defense and "peace-keeping" forays.

In a Sunday School class, shortly after the Palestinian slaughter, several troubled Bible students asked, "If we say Israel is God's chosen people, just how far should we as Christians support them?"

I believe there are ample grounds to argue against the resolution: "Because of the biblical promises, Christians have an obligation to insure the future well-being of Israel."

At least four critical reasons call for Christians to review their alleged duties to preserve the nation of Israel. (1) The New Testament Christian revelation of love condemns some Israeli methods. (2) God himself has often withheld support from His covenant people. (3) Israel's survival really hinges on how they handle the question: "Who is Jesus?" (4) The ultimate defense of God's people is not arms and military might, but through faith in His divine triumph.

First, concern to preserve Israel often finds Israeli methods in conflict with Christian goals of reconciliation. To give the nation of Israel *carte blanche* approval is irresponsible. God's covenant with Abraham and his seed (see Genesis 13, 15, 17) was made in divine foreknowledge, but not without terms. Their inheritance required individual and collective faith and obedience.

Second, God himself did not support His covenant people when they disobeyed. Though He delivered the Israelites from Egyptian slavery (Exodus 6—12), disobedience barred them from the Promised Land. They wandered in the wilderness for 40 years.

A new generation of people followed God's man, Joshua, across the Jordan River, and into their promised possession. But after the mighty walled city of Jericho fell, the children of Israel met humiliating defeat at Ai. The land could not be obtained without faithful obedience to God.

Now, as then, God deals with people both as a nation and as individuals. Despite Israel's frequent rejection, God has always had a people responding to His prophetic call. Our time is no different. All peoples, whether Jews, Arabs, or Gentile Christians, must give a strict account. Biblical promises do not absolve anyone from loyalty to God.

Third, more vital than armaments to Israel's survival is how they answer the question: "Who is Jesus?" Israel's present assignment as God's chosen people depends on a remnant that accepts God's Messiah. Though Jews generally rejected Christ, Gentiles believed and claimed God's salvation promise.

By faith, the Church inherits the kingdom of God. This does not cancel the role of the Jew, nor demote their standing before God. The ultimate triumph of God's people, Jew and Gentile, requires constant faith in Jesus as the Christ, the Savior, and coming King.

God has had a plan for His people, Israel. Gentile nations have been used to help bring it to pass. Cyrus, the Persian, was moved to restore Judah to their homeland, releasing them from Babylonian captivity (Isaiah 45). For a time their hopes remained alive, until doubts and sin prevailed.

In 1918, upon Turkey's defeat in World War I, England established the Protectorate of Palestine. Allied victory in World War II set the stage for the renewal of the nation of Israel after a lapse of over 1,900 years. From Jerusalem's destruction by the Romans in A.D. 70, till May of 1948, God seemed aloof.

Meanwhile, the Nazi Germany program from 1938 classified Jews as a vermin race, and slaughtered over 6 million by the war's end in 1945. The official response of the Christian Church to the Holocaust ranged from silence to mild protest. People had supposed that this judgment came to the Jews for crucifying Jesus.

The Church absorbed guilt for the Holocaust as it ignored the plight of the Jews. That blame cannot be erased by providing a stockpile of arms for Israel's defense now. Today, the Church risks committing the error of neglecting the human needs of Palestinian Arabs who have come under the rule of Israel.

In the final analysis, armed might will neither save individual Jews nor insure their well-being as a nation. Their security is gained only by turning to Christ.

Christ commissioned His Church to be witnesses to all peoples. That takes priority to the political defense of the Jews. Israel, at present, is not a God-led nation. Thus, any concern for their military strength must not foreclose the Christian message to the Palestinian Arabs and others of the Middle East. Israel will succeed only as she receives God's Messiah.

The true obligation of Christians is to be instruments of

God, not "lord-protectors" of Israel. The future of Israel as a nation remains in the hands of her own people in relation to God.

## Reaction and Rebuttal

Some time ago the speaker at the National Association of Arab Americans said, "We wish <u>FOR</u> the members in Congress would stop believing fairy tales about the Middle East, such as the biblical right of the Jewish people to Palestine."

This reveals the basic truth of the Middle East problem. To the Muslim, the Bible is not an authority. Only the Koran is true. But to the Christian, the Bible is the inspired Word of God, which declares that Palestine belongs to the Jews and that nations will be judged on their attitudes toward Israel.

The Middle East problem, to a great extent, is religious. It stems from Abraham's effort to fulfill God's promise by having a son by Hagar, Sarah's handmaid. The consequence of that act is even today being reflected in the current animosity between the children of Isaac (Israel) and the children of Ishmael (the Arabs).

Today, Ishmael's line claims the Promised Land as their own because they claim descendancy from Abraham, as does Israel. Both are descendants, but God's covenant is with Isaac (Genesis 17:20-21).

The arguments author Beals points out are valid as far as they go; however, there is a bigger issue at stake.

The decision to support Israel cannot be made on human reasoning, but on the basis of Scripture and on God's covenant with Abraham. That covenant declares God will single out Israel and use her to fulfill His plan for the world.

In spite of Israel's mistakes and disobedience, the Jews are God's chosen people. And He promised to grant them the restoration of their land and influence throughout the world. He is fulfilling that promise now. As a result, Israel deserves our attention and support.

$T$HE BIBLICAL PROMISES to Israel, and to **AGAINST** Christians, are not unconditional. They demand personal trust in God. At least three points qualify the ties between Christians and modern Jews:

*Christians cannot really insure the future well-being of Israel.* This is because Israel, "chosen by God" to bear the promised Messiah, refused Jesus Christ. And so God opened His salvation covenant to include the Gentiles. All believers, as spiritual Israel, are "chosen" to inherit the promise and become witnesses (Romans 10:12-13). Physical Israel must accept God's Messiah to fulfill its prophetic role.

*Christians are called of God to build His spiritual kingdom.* Salvation is not merely for physical Israel. It is for all believers: spiritual Israel. God's love flows through His people to Jews, and to all the rest of mankind.

*Christians who "stand with Israel" are not necessarily standing with God.* Support of modern Israel is no sure sign a Christian is pleasing God. God wants people to turn from sin. So His solution to evil is more than a political compact between nations. God's people must hold His Word in faith to be kingdom-heirs with Christ.

Jesus' Great Commission to His disciples was to preach repentance and forgiveness of sins, in His name, among all nations (see Luke 24:47-49; Acts 1:9-11). This divine command to evangelize all nations remains the prime task of all Christians. Fulfilling this command, more than developing political ties with the physical state of Israel, is what God wants of His followers—the new Israel.

---

1. Richard W. DeHaan, *Israel: the Apple of God's Eye* (Grand Rapids: Radio Bible Class, 1983), 5-6.

2. Charles C. Ryrie, *The Basis of the Premillennial Faith* (New York: Loizeaux Brothers, 1953), 50-52.

*C. D. Hansen is a pastor in Rochester, N.Y.*

*Ivan A. Beals is office editor for the* Herald of Holiness, *Kansas City.*

## Chapter 7

*The Issue:*

# Divorce

*Statement for Debate:*

**Divorce is an acceptable option for the Christian.**

by

Harold Ivan Smith (For)

Paul Merritt Bassett (Against)

*Background Scripture:*

**Matthew 18:21-35; 19:1-12**

O NCE UPON A TIME the Christian home | **FOR** |
seemed immune from divorce—"a haven in a
heartless world." But is any home safe when divorce claims 1.8
million marriages each year?

Christians are divorcing. That reality no doubt prompts
this debate.

Once we lived in small, tight communities where social
stigma prevailed. The church, acting with other social institutions, had enough power to force a couple to remain married.
The sacraments could be denied the divorced—particularly
"the guilty party." How often we made it our business to find
out who that party was!

Preachers warned of dire consequences to the children
who came "from a broken home." At least they did until researchers concluded that children from an unstable home suf-
fered even more. Christians threatened the divorced with not
only consequences in this world but hell in the next. However,

"We don't believe in divorce—
We'll just stay in there and keep punching."

the general decline in that doctrine, in favor of the more comforting "God is a good God who loves you," has sapped our persuasive threats of their vitality.

I believe that divorce is an acceptable option for Christians. This statement excludes an opinion on the controversial question of remarriage, since it is not included in the proposition we are debating.

Paul wrote, *"If it is possible* [which implied there are times when it is not], as far as it depends on you, live at peace with everyone" (Romans 12:18). When we debate this issue, we must leave behind our image of the ideal family. This is because Christians live, love, marry, grieve, and survive in a real world. Sadly, some people cannot be lived with.

In a world where alcoholism touches one in five adults;

In a world of drug addiction and substance abuse;

In a world of rampant mental stress and illness;

In a world where homosexuals marry, attempting to convert to heterosexuality or to hide their sexual preference;

In a world where in-laws foster an ongoing relationship with a married son or daughter, contrary to Scripture;

We must sadly admit "divorce is an acceptable option."

However, we must ask, "What is marriage?" Are two people "doomed" to live out a lifetime of second-choice because they spoke a foolish "I do"? And how many were forced or coerced to say "I do"? How many were *pushed* into love before they had a chance to fall in love?

Jesus' verbal handslap of the Pharisees who questioned Him on divorce is appropriate for some church members today (Mark 10:1-5). The only difference between today's Pharisee and the original Pharisees is that contemporary Pharisees wear permanent press and Aqua Velva or Avon. Armed with a scattering of proof texts, statistics, and "my Bible says," they descend on the divorced with a hurricanelike intensity that contradicts Paul's clear teaching in Galatians 6:1-2.

In responding to the Pharisees, Jesus said, "a man will leave his father and mother" (Mark 10:7). Researchers and pastoral counselors are discovering that a significant number of divorces are caused by interfering in-laws, particularly moth-ers-in-law. The vow says, "forsaking *all* others."

Secondly, Jesus' words "what God has joined together, let man not separate" (Matthew 19:6) are frequently paraphrased in wedding ceremonies—but unfortunately with a tardy emphasis. The stress should be on the *first* phrase, "what God has joined," unless we dare to suggest that *anyone* who has ever said "I do" is married in God's sight.

Certainly, divorce must always be the last stop on a long journey. It comes after more than just "the straw that breaks the camel's back." Divorce comes only after prayer, suffering, counseling, and separation. Jesus' tough words on divorce in Matthew 19 are preceded by His equally tough words on forgiveness in Matthew 18.

The wedding vows should be entered into advisedly, reverently, discreetly, and in the fear of God. The same should be characteristic of the decision to divorce. Divorce must never be an idle threat or an attempt "to force" the mate to "straighten up and fly right." Divorce is a confession, however painful, that two people have failed.

Too often, in the name of Jesus, righteousness, and carnal pride, we have encouraged, even forced, some people to remain in comatose marriages that exist only by the mechanical support of a piece of paper.

How easily and pridefully we proclaim, "Thank God I'm not like those who are divorced!" I have not forgotten the woman who boldly declared, "Bless God, I took my vows seriously!" but has made every day of her husband's life miserable.

Divorce statistics do not reveal the tragic, long history of questionable annulments, homicides, suicides, mental breakdowns, and trumped-up commitments to mental hospitals—"remedies" once pervasive in a society that had a low divorce rate.

Finally, the church must foster a portion of the blame. When two-thirds of our church members receive no premarital counseling, when most premarital counseling is in fact preceremonial counseling, when too many Christians think marital counseling is "for other people," when Christians think an

"I do" legitimizes sexual relations, when a tragic percentage of teens and young adults marry on a hormonal instinct and dare to quote Paul's "it is better to marry than to burn," the church must be reluctant to condemn anyone.

Whose fault is the lack of counseling: the couple, or a church that rationalizes, "If we don't marry them, someone else will"?

If the church were really being the church, and really taking marriage seriously, divorce would be a rare option.

I dislike divorce. But I minister in a real world where people make commitments and decisions that veto previous relationships.

Divorce, I must reluctantly conclude, is an acceptable although regrettable option that causes the church to grieve.

**D**IVORCE is not an acceptable option for the **AGAINST** Christian. But we have to qualify this.

First, let's do our biblical homework, beginning in Genesis. There we read about the creation and pairing of man and woman, and the story of their fall into sin. Genesis 1:26-31 focuses on the couple's responsibility to reproduce and to govern the rest of creation. And Genesis 2:18-25 underlines their relationship to each other. They are to become "one flesh."

But then comes the Fall. Instead of becoming "one flesh" they act independently, then blame each other for their respective predicaments. And the deepest symbol of their unity, and the means for expressing it, becomes a source of shame to them. They were now naked and ashamed. So with "fig leaves" they try to hide their bodies from one another. God had created them for unity, though they were different. Disunited, they try now to hide the differences.

Their "fig leaves" are inappropriate, apparently, because God himself clothes them. But in doing this He is not accepting things as they are. This is adaptation, divine adjustment to human tragedy. Graciously, He protects them from the fury of the punishment their folly called for.

God's strategy ever since has been full of gracious concessions to us in our mess. Much of biblical law itself relates to divine adaptation and concession. It does not express God's original intention, His perfect will.

That's why Paul says that the law was "added" (Galatians 3:19). And in Romans 7, he teaches us that it has a threefold design: bringing us to know our utter sinfulness, frustrating our attempts to save ourselves by obeying it, and compelling us to fling ourselves, in trust, on Christ for salvation.

This helps us understand Jesus' earlier response to the Pharisees' question about divorce (Matthew 19:3-9; Mark 10:2-12). Actually, their question is a test case, an illustration, meant to show that Jesus was disrespectful of the law and at the same time too idealistic in His teaching concerning the ethic of the kingdom of heaven. So, He agrees: Moses, divinely guided, permitted divorce (Deuteronomy 24:1-4). But, He insists, this was not God's original intention. God responded to our "hardness of heart" with another divine concession. In the kingdom of heaven, present even on earth, the original intention still holds: marriage is indissoluble.

Divorce is but a graciously granted concession. "But from the beginning it has not been this way." The concession is permitted to keep people from damaging each other even more than they do.

Matthew shows the disciples fretting: "Better not to marry if marriage is indissoluble and divorce but a concession to hardness of heart." And Jesus says, "Correct. You will need grace, single or married" (Matthew 19:10-12, writer's paraphrase).

He has already insisted that true disciples live above concessions allowed for hardness of heart. They are to exercise the Kingdom's ethic and the Father's perfection (see Matthew 5—7).

That's a brief look at the biblical evidence.

Now, before drawing our conclusion, let's clarify the terms of the debate itself.

*First,* the issue is divorce, not the more serious matter of remarriage.

*Second,* our subject is Christian—not pagan, not nominal Christian. This person gives allegiance to the kingdom of heaven, knows Christ as Lord, and accepts the Scriptures as the sole rule for faith and practice. We're assuming that the person considering divorce (1) has already been converted and (2) really has a choice.

*Third,* the issue is "acceptability"; and we're assuming that the question "Acceptable to whom?" is answered "To the Christian who is considering divorce and who is answerable to God."

The first two points may be useful. But it is the third one that is critical to the debate.

By any dictionary definition, *acceptable* is a positive word. It includes the ideas "worth accepting," "satisfactory" and "adequate." And it is precisely this positive character that moves us to reject the notion that divorce is "an acceptable option" for the Christian.

Divorce is certainly not worth accepting. There is nothing good about it. The best that can be said for it is that it may be less bad in some circumstances than any other alternative.

Nor is it "satisfactory." For the Christian, "satisfactory," applied to human relations, translates into love and reconciliation. So, divorce is never satisfactory. In fact, it may sometimes be the least of the unsatisfactory alternatives.

"Adequate" divorce is not. Actually, it testifies to inadequacy—to hardness of heart.

So, given the human mess, divorce may be permitted, or admissible. But it is not acceptable for the Christian. We have to be careful not to confuse God's concession with His intention. His gracious concession, to protect us from the full effects of our own sinfulness, may help us to see into the depths of human meanness. It should lead us to know and yearn to do His perfect will. We must not exercise divorce and then argue for its goodness as if it were the very will of God. At best, it is but the least bad among alternatives.

We err tragically if we refuse the graciousness of the concession by defending our exercise of divorce as a good.

We are on our way to health if, having become divorced, we seek and accept God's forgiveness and that of the Church and then commit ourselves to obeying His "good and acceptable and perfect will." Humble ourselves we must; grovel we need not. Presume upon His grace we dare not; appropriate it we shall—all of us.

So, divorce really is an unacceptable, though admissable, option for the Christian.

## Reaction and Rebuttal

**M**R. BASSETT has offered what appears, on the surface, to be a compassionate case for rejecting divorce as an acceptable option. However, he has sidestepped the real issue: is or is not divorce acceptable—by focusing on one word in the proposition that he defines as "worth accepting," "satisfactory," or "adequate."

FOR

He confesses that "the best that can be said for *it* is that *it* may be less bad in some circumstances than any other alternative"—twice avoiding the word *divorce*. However, as I originally noted, family violence and homicide are among the alternatives to divorce. Taking Bassett's criteria, we must ask,

"Is family violence *worth accepting?*"

"Is family violence *satisfactory?*"

"Is family violence *adequate?*"

Going one step further, is the church's stance that divorce is *not* an option *(a)* worth accepting? *(b)* satisfactory? or *(c)* adequate? No, because such an attitude condemns believers who are trapped in traumatic marriages to seek their own solutions.

In an era of family violence, when thousands of mates are shot or knifed rather than divorced, when children lose a parent in death and a second one to prison, we have sabotaged a generation because we have judged divorce an unacceptable option.

In order to "serve the present age" we must learn to accept those forced into divorce by circumstances we may never understand and by sin. And we must do this without incarcerating them in a lifetime guaranteed spiritual straightjacket of neo-leprosy.

We must never allow those who have made "unacceptable" choices to be forever branded as unacceptable in the body of believers.

$M$R. SMITH reviewed important facts about **AGAINST** divorce among Christians: the church has sometimes mishandled divorce; the world is morally rotten; some "I dos" were foolishly vowed; Pharisees, ancient and modern, torment those who are divorced; in-laws often interfere in marriages; some marriages lack divine sanction; Christian social pressure has inhibited the dissolution of harmful marriages; self-righteous spouses can create marital misery; the low divorce rates of the past hide some of the real story; and the church often fails in both premarital counseling and coping with divorce.

These facts must not be ignored. But they only describe the context; describing the context and responding to the question "is divorce acceptable for the Christian" are two very different—though related—matters. Describing the patient's surroundings, or even the symptoms, does not answer the question about the acceptability of the proposed surgery.

The world's bias against marital stability, human cussedness, and the church's failures may help explain why there is divorce—but these are not arguments for its *acceptability*. They are arguments that guarantee there will be divorce, not that divorce is satisfactory or adequate.

Christians want to meet God's *intention*. But divorce, says Scripture, is God's *concession*. Falling back on the concession instead of conforming to the divine intention cannot be *acceptable* to God or to believers.

At best, it can be argued that in this fallen world divorce seems necessary—a divinely provided way of keeping us from doing even more harm to each other than we do.

*Harold Ivan Smith is a frequent lecturer at singles retreats and an author of several books on divorce. He is divorced and lives in Kansas City.*
*Paul Merritt Bassett is professor of the history of Christianity at Nazarene Theological Seminary, Kansas City.*

## Chapter 8

*The Issue:*

# Is Economic Growth Progress?

*Statement for Debate:*

**Economic growth is progress.**

by

Robert Hubbard (For)

Edwin R. Squiers (Against)

*Background Scripture:*

**Genesis 1:26-31; Isaiah 56:9-12; 1 Timothy 5:8**

$E$CONOMIC GROWTH really is progress, in spite of what the environmentalists say.

> FOR

But you might not agree with this—at least until you have taken a hard look at some of the basic principles that are fundamental to our economy.

First, natural resources that provide us with goods and services are diminishing through use.

Second, the wants of mankind greatly exceed resources available to provide for these wants.

Third, this tension between limited resources and unlimited wants means we have to make choices about how to use the resources to satisfy the wants. The dilemma we face is this: how far can we go in striving for economic growth before we become foolish and unethical in dealing with the environment?

Society has tried many ways to make the right economic and environmental decisions. In today's world there are two basic systems that exist to make these choices. One is a centralized body of individuals who decides for a whole society, such as we find in the Soviet Union and Cuba. The other is a free market system that operates on the uncoordinated actions of all people within the society and who, by supply and demand, decide what will or will not be bought and sold. Examples of this system include North America, Western Europe, and Japan.

The three fundamental economic principles we mentioned clearly suggest that humanity requires continuous economic growth in order to meet the consumption demands of the group.

It is tempting to identify "economic wants" as all the negative things Christians normally reject: unnecessary material goods, excessive consumption, indulgence in luxuries, and other self-serving objectives.

But, first of all, Luke 16:13 makes it clear that the issue is not that we have abundance but what we do with that abundance. And in the second place, economic wants are generally the basic elements required to grow a quality life: opportunity for work; money to house, feed, and clothe our families; care for

our churches and colleges; essential material goods and professional services; health care and retirement needs. Even Christians hope for some level of comfort in this portion of the eternal pilgrimage. And for us to pursue these most basic interests, we must have a growing economy.

But our growing economy has placed such a strain on the environment that the tension between it and economic growth has become one of the crucial issues of the century. Some of the questions raised include:

- Should we continue production in technologies that appear to create acid rain, which conservative environmentalists claim ruins water supplies and kills animal life?
- Should we continue to increase production as a way of providing employment, or should we tolerate higher levels of unemployment to lessen the severity of pollution?
- Is economic growth and progress one and the same?

The answer to these and similar questions must be yes. Economic growth must continue, in spite of the recognized impact on the environment, lest we totally upset an economy that has become so complex it forever teeters on the ledge of recession. This complexity comes from the fact that we are no longer independent, but are influenced in our economic decisions by what happens in other parts of the world. If our economy slows down, or stops growing, the impact is worldwide.

I would further suggest that economic deregulation is required in order to permit the necessary growth in our economy. Incentives such as tax relief can be made available to industries that take steps to conserve energy. Federal lands can be opened for additional exploration of untapped energy sources. Various government agencies that now keep a lid on economic growth by artificial means, such as legislative controls, can be eliminated, saving millions of dollars in wasteful expense. At the same time, we can parallel economic production with research to generate new ways of producing goods and services with new forms of energy such as solar energy from the sun, thermal energy from the hot water beneath the earth's surface, and nuclear energy from the basic building blocks of matter.

Growth is essential in the physical world. Growth is one of the indisputable laws of God, and we emphasize this in our religious practices. Consider such phrases as "growing in the Spirit" and "growth in grace." Preventing growth, in either religion or economics, is tantamount to announcing an impending death.

In reality, we cannot argue "use fewer resources," for it is an unchangeable fact that it takes resources to produce goods or services for the benefit of humanity. We should accept that someday coal and oil will be used up, trees will be fewer in number, and other resources will also be diminished. The task for the Christian is to actively support the best possible methods of using available resources, while recognizing that a position to slow down or reverse the process of growth is counterproductive in today's world. The issue for the Christian is not to choose between "growth" and "no growth." Growth is a must. Rather, the emphasis should be placed on (1) making scripturally informed choices about identifying proper social goals and (2) properly managing the waste spun off in the process of achieving those goals through production.

It is not the slowing down of growth that will save the environment; it will be in using our God-given intelligence to manage the consequences of our productive acts.

As Christians, we must do our best to live up to 1 Timothy 5:8, which makes a strong case for growth through work and use of available resources, in order to enable us to care for our immediate and extended family. And we cannot stop there. Growth is not only a concern for this day and age, it is an intergenerational issue. What we are, and what we have, rests on the backs of those who have labored before us. As they grew, we have grown; as we grow, so may those who come after us.

It is the mismanagement of the by-products of growth, or pollution, that now captures our attention. Given this, we must now focus on growth in ways that resolve the by-product issues.

And so, it must be held that economic growth, even in the fact of diminishing resources and inadequate handling of waste by-products, is progress.

Genesis 1:26-31 indicates we are accountable for the ways we transform nature to care for our needs. Throughout Scripture, our role in this world is described as "stewardship"—and progress is an essential element of good stewardship. Through economic growth we experience increases in prosperity. And if this prosperity is used as scripture demands, it will provide increased service within the Church, and to those who need to be fed and clothed before they can confront their own spiritual needs and claim the promises of Jesus Christ.

THE NOTION that economic growth is progress **AGAINST** is so much a part of modern culture that few of us even give it a second thought. We live in a society where the goal of materialism permeates every aspect of our lives. To have is to be.

The difference between "I need" and "I want" is blurred beyond recognition, and the concept of "enough" is all but lost. We support a multibillion-dollar, need-creating industry called "advertising," which constantly tells us that things bring happiness. "Buy, possess, and accumulate, then you will be complete, happy, and fulfilled."

Economic growth is progress—or so says society. "Production, purchase, and ownership—that's the way to the good life." A materialistic world demands a tangible basis for personal worth, and so economic growth becomes the measure of progress. This equation for progress has become so much a part of our thinking that we believe economic growth is not only a necessity but also a birthright that can and must persist. Woe unto the man who stands in the way of "progress."

My dictionary defines *progress* as "a moving forward toward perfection, an advance toward the goal." Therefore, whether or not economic growth is progress depends largely on your goal. Although life is full of secondary goals, all of them relate to one of two ultimate goals toward which we progress.

Paul, the apostle, summarized these utlimate goals in his letter to the Philippians. We may choose to serve God as we "press on toward the goal to win the prize for which God has called me heavenward in Christ Jesus" (3:14). Or we may serve ourselves as "enemies of the cross of Christ: whose end is destruction, whose God is their belly, and whose glory is in their shame, who mind earthly things" (3:18-19, KJV).

Satan offered Adam this choice in the Garden: serve the Creator, or serve yourself—serve God, or try to be god. All that we say, all that we do, and all that we are moves us closer to one or the other of these two goals.

You can't have it both ways. You cannot move toward two major goals at the same time. In the sixth chapter of Matthew, Jesus makes it clear that we are all slaves to something, or someone. "No one can serve two masters. Either he will hate the one and love the other, or he will be devoted to the one and despise the other. You cannot serve both God and Money" (v. 24).

Whether or not economic growth is progress is largely determined by which goal we press toward. "For where your treasure is, there your heart will be also" (Matthew 6:21). Do we serve God and do His will, or do we serve ourselves by the accumulation of earthly riches?

Money is not evil. But it is dangerous because more often than not it displaces God at the center of our lives. Although Jesus never condemned wealth, He often reminded His followers of the perils of seeking after financial gain and the false sense of security that comes if it is attained. In Luke 12:15 He instructed His disciples, "Watch out! Be on your guard against all kinds of greed; a man's life does not consist in the abundance of his possessions."

As humans, we are tempted to pursue security in the context of economic growth. Like the "successful" farmer in the parable, we build bigger barns in order to keep our possessions while saying, "Soul, you have ample goods laid up for many years; take your ease, eat, drink, be merry" (Luke 12:19, RSV).

We are so busy with the pursuit of more, so busy serving self, that we fail to hear God respond, "You fool!" The man who lays up treasure for himself is not rich toward God.

The real danger is not that the world believes economic growth is progress. The real danger comes when that notion permeates the Church as well—when Satan's lie lures us into satisfaction in serving ourselves. And the real danger flourishes when we continue to deceive ourselves by talking of heaven while we strive for "mammon."

Growth economics is a mythical paradox—two opposites: it is, on one hand, too materialistic and, on the other hand, not materialistic enough. The notions of justice, equity, and quality of life go largely unnoticed, while progress is measured in the dollar value of the Gross National Product. Ethics and the ultimate ends of the Creator are ignored, thus growth economics is too materialistic. At the other end of the spectrum, growth economics is also found wanting. By ignoring the limited nature of the Creation and the findings of the young science of ecology, growth economics is not "materialistic" enough. Yet, we pursue the illusion with gusto—the illusion of gain without pain—the illusion of the free lunch.

In a culture that is so completely engulfed by materialism, we must ask ourselves: What goal do we strive for? Whom do we serve? Are we selling our souls for an illusion of security? Are we selling our souls for a myth of progress?

> Yea, they are greedy dogs which can never have enough, and they are shepherds that cannot understand: they all look to their own way, every one for his gain, from his quarter. Come ye, say they, I will fetch wine, and we will fill ourselves with strong drink; and to morrow shall be as this day, and much more abundant *(Isaiah 56:11-12, KJV)*.

"Come ye," they say, "economic growth is progress." Thus we are deceived, and thus we deceive ourselves.

## Reaction and Rebuttal

**W**HEN MY OPPONENT in this debate compares economic growth to materialism, he falls $\boxed{\textbf{FOR}}$ into the common trap of oversimplifying the issue. I am not arguing that we should be valued by what we have.

Both economic growth and materialism can be overdone. In fact, true economic growth often requires a reduction in materialism. Society requires growth to meet its many needs.

It is not economic growth that is the culprit in this discussion. The "bad" part of economic growth has to do with what one does with his abundance. What is interesting is that within the church there always seems to be someone who knows better than ourselves what exactly is "enough" for us.

Greed exists both in and out of the church. I'm just glad it is God who judges the heart, and what we do with the fruits of economic growth. And I'm glad it's not the conservationists (theological and otherwise) who acknowledge that economic growth can provide for life's needs, but who are doing little to solve the real problems of waste by-products produced in the growth process.

$F$OUR IDEAS of the opposing argument demand **AGAINST** response.

First, "Growth is essential in the physical world." In fact, it is balance—not growth—that is essential in the created order. When one thing gains, something else loses. One is born, as another dies. One grows only if another decays. When the balance is lost, the system collapses. The same is true of man's economics. When we gain, we must ask, "Who loses?" Only God's infinite nature makes unlimited growth possible in the spiritual realm.

Second, growth must continue "for the benefit of humanity." While we in the "First World" have benefited from economic growth, the evidence is overwhelming that both the gap between rich and poor and the sum total of human misery are greater today than ever before. The claim that growth gives us more to share with others, is not supported. In reality, if I get more, chances are I'll keep it.

Third, economic growth must continue regardless of the impact on the environment because if it stops, the world economic system will fail. In fact, short-term "ignore-ance" of environmental problems in favor of economic growth is "penny-wise and pound-foolish." As devastating as economic collapse might be, it would be minor compared to the global impact of a major ecological collapse.

Finally, the classic argument—"Everybody else has one . . . I *need* one too!" My nine-year-old uses it to plead for the latest "necessary" toy. My opponent uses it more to justify economic order to meet the consumption demands of the group. Either form sounds hauntingly like Aaron's explanation to Moses of the golden calf: "I only gave them what they wanted." Scripture warns us not to assume that actions are justified by popular vote. We must take great care not to proclaim the demands of the group as "right" nor the convenient as "holy."

The notion that "economic growth is progress" is a seductive trap, and we must take care not to be deceived by it.

*Robert Hubbard is chairman of the Department of Business Administration at Eastern Nazarene College, Quincy, Mass.*

*Edwin R. Squiers is a professor of advanced courses in ecology, environmental analysis, and ethics at Taylor University, Upland, Ind.*

## Chapter 9

*The Issue:*

# Equality for Women

*Statement for Debate:*

**Evangelical Christians, of all people, should support equality for women.**

by

Ann C. Rearick (For)

Jamieline Johnson (Against)

*Background Scripture:*

**Galatians 3:26-29; 1 Timothy 2:9-14**

Since evangelicals want to follow the teachings of God's Word, they of all people [ **FOR** ] should support equality for women.

Here is what God's Word says in Genesis 1:26-27, "Then God said, 'Let us make man in our image, in our likeness, and let them rule over the fish of the sea and the birds of the air, over the livestock, over all the earth, and all the creatures that move along the ground.' So God created man in his own image, in the image of God he created him; male and female he created them."

These verses show that both men and women were created in the image of God. And there is no evidence that the attributes of God were divided between them with those of emotional stability, logical thinking, and intelligence going primarily to males. In addition we see that both man and woman were to rule over the creation God had given them.

"The last time I was equal to her
was when we were both standing on top of the wedding cake."

In the second chapter of Genesis we see the response of Adam to the mate God had given him. We can sense his delight with his words, "This is now bone of my bones and flesh of my flesh" (2:23).

Writing about this passage, Adam Clarke, the great commentator of the evangelical revival, says, "As God formed her out of a part of the man himself, he saw she was of the same nature, the same identical flesh and blood, and of the same constitution in all respects, and consequently having equal powers, faculties, and rights. This at once insured his affection, and excited his esteem."

Some have taken Genesis 2:18, "And the Lord God said, 'It is not good for the man to be alone. I will make a helper suitable for him,'" to mean that Adam was to be in charge while Eve was to help him in his tasks. In other words, Eve was to be his subordinate. There is no basis for this according to the word usage of the Old Testament. *Ezer,* used as a noun meaning "help" or "helper," appears 21 times in the Old Testament. Sixteen of these refer to a *super*ordinate helper, not a *sub*ordinate.

"Where does my help come from? My help comes from the Lord," says Psalm 121:1-2. Psalm 146:5 tells us, "Blessed is he whose help is the God of Jacob." At no time is *ezer* used to indicate a subordinate helper unless the references in Genesis 2 are taken to be exceptions to the general rule.[1]

But inequality came on the scene because of sin. Genesis 3:16 says, "Your desire will be for your husband, and he will rule over you." This happened. Women became possessions, considered to be inferior to men. In fact, tradition teaches that Jewish men thanked God each morning that they weren't dogs, Gentiles, or women.

So, those who quote Genesis 3:16 as a basis for men ruling women are mistaken. The verse is a proclamation of what happened because of sin—it is not a statement of what God intended. Nowhere in Scripture is this verse used to prove that women should be subordinated.[2]

In the New Testament, John tells us that "the reason the Son of God appeared was to destroy the devil's work" (1 John 3:8). Since the subjection of women came about as the result of sin, this is one of the works Jesus came to destroy. And in His life we see this happening.

Jesus didn't treat women in a manner usual for His day. The Samaritan woman was amazed that He would even speak to her—but He went beyond just chatting. He talked of eternal things.

As another example, Mary was commended for wanting to sit at the feet of Jesus and listen. She was not treated with condescension but as a human being wanting to learn. And this was in a day when rabbis would not teach women since they were considered incapable of grasping theological truth.

A clear teaching of Jesus is that one person is not to subject another. In Mark 10:42-44 He said, "You know that those who are regarded as rulers of the Gentiles lord it over them, and their high officials exercise authority over them. Not so with you. Instead, whoever wants to become great among you must be your servant, and whoever wants to be first must be slave of all." We are not to look for ways to rule, but for ways to serve.

With the coming of the Holy Spirit, equality is restored even more. In Acts 1 and 2 we see that the Holy Spirit fell on women just as He did on men. Furthermore, Peter acknowledged that what was happening had been foretold by the prophet Joel when he said that God would pour out His Spirit on *all* people, and both sons and daughters would prophesy.

The church is the loser when women are not considered equal with men.

In 1 Corinthians after listing gifts given by the Holy Spirit, Paul says, "But one and the same Spirit works all these things, distributing to each one individually just as He wills" (12:11, NASB). Some would even then deny women the opportunity to use the gifts God has given them. A woman is encouraged to use the gift of helping, but not that of administration, teaching (especially teaching men), or preaching.

Research has shown that "women who do not use their gifts are often bound by frustration, lack of fulfillment, and even guilt."[3] When the Bible doesn't differentiate between gifts for men and for women, how can we?

It is interesting that in times of revival in the history of

Christianity, women and men alike sense a call to ministry. But when the revival spirit dies, the male hierarchy of the church takes control.[4]

The present-day reluctance of evangelicals not to support equality for women is probably a backlash to the extremes of the "Women's Lib" movement. But let us not allow our reaction to extremes to keep us from supporting the biblical view of equality for women.

IN THE LAST 20 YEARS the cry for "equality for women" has blasted us from every direction— **AGAINST** the media, colleges, government, social organizations, and even churches. This cry comes not from God but from the selfish humanity that has caused the inequality in the first place. The volumes that have been written and spoken about this capitalize the "me." And the whole impact is that "me" and "my equality" come before "you" and "your equality."

The demand is rooted in a selfish desire fed by Satan, who from the very beginning has tried to overthrow God and His design for this world. Therefore, we cannot subscribe to the statement "that evangelical Christians, of all people, should support equality for women."

All you have to do to reveal this mind-set as anti-Christian is to review some of the demands by modern feminists. Although they sound appealing, when you look at them from a biblical perspective, they are anti-God and an attempt to destroy God's design for the sexes. They picture God as a male-biased power that delights in keeping woman in her place. Attacks are leveled at facts such as the two separate sexes and their roles, the institution of marriage, and even the traditional family. The end—equality—is the goal. And it doesn't matter what it takes to get there. The fair-sounding phrase, "equality for women," has at its core the desire to overthrow God's authority and pattern for life. It means, "I want to be in complete control of my body and me." But a Christian must allow God to have complete control—selfishly motivated desires should not replace Him at the helm.

Many who seek equality for women have said men and women are basically the same, despite the biological differences. Masculine and feminine traits, they say, are culturally induced and should be disregarded. A feminine nature is seen as something negative, so it should be ignored. Feminist writers almost seem to hate the female sex. A woman must think, act, talk, and react like a man if she is to reach equality. But the fact is, she loses her freedom to be a woman when she feels she must be as a man.

Another thing she loses is sight of God's plan for woman. The creation story reveals the characteristics that the male and female have in common and those that are different (Genesis 1—2). The woman was designed to help man, for example, as a wife and a mother if she chose marriage. From hairstyle to career, the goal of the equality movement is to blend the sexes into a unisex. Christians must resist an equality that has come to mean sameness without acknowledgement of different roles for the sexes.

Another problem with the "equality" movement is that it threatens the institution of marriage because it accepts lesbian relationships. A possible marriage contract with the same sex is proposed to assure equality. Christians cannot be a part of any movement that approves of sexual relationships that go against God's design for man and woman (Matthew 19:4-6).

In a related attack, feminists make a mockery of the traditional family life-style. We are led to believe that being a "housewife" is a demeaning, confining, and valueless role. No challenge is seen in the role of nurturing of children. In fact, these people have applied political pressure to force the government to establish federally funded child care centers so women can have the freedom to "find themselves" in careers outside the home. So while adult females seek their creative individual goals, their child females will be forced to live their most formative years in an environment that stifles creativity because of established guidelines that encourage sameness.

Under Christ's leadership there is room for a two-career family. But the motive of such a plan is vitally important. The soaring divorce rate among "church" couples in recent years gives evidence of misguided desires. If "equality" means destruction of the family, it cannot be in God's will.

Perhaps the most heartbreaking result of the equality for woman movement is destruction of life through abortion. When we abort a child for convenience' sake, as a way to exercise control of our body and life, we become enemies of the biblical teaching of life's value. Christians must oppose any movement that encourages such a tactic. We, of all people, know the value of life. After all, Christ came and died for us to have life (John 3:16; 10:10).

Equality for women has become an end that is sought whatever the means. The "me" is placed before God and family. The motivation is supported with misplaced values that oppose biblical principles laid down for us in God's Word. Feminism, like humanism, removes God from the center of the universe. But while humanism places mankind in the center, feminism puts woman in the center. Christians recognize that God is the center not only of the universe but also of life. An idealogy that seeks to replace God with self must be rejected.

As committed Christians we must fulfill God's design for our life, which we attain through Jesus Christ who gives to all people a status of worth beyond anything that selfish humanity can offer (Galatians 3:28).

Man's selfishness, not God's plan, produced inequality.


## Reaction and Rebuttal

THE "CRY FOR EQUALITY" comes not from "selfish humanity," as Mrs. Johnson puts it, but | FOR | from a deep-seated principle God has built into each one of us: the need to be free to be what He wants us to be. The priesthood of all believers, the "all one in Christ Jesus" is possible only when we consider one another as equals.

While recognizing the evil and selfishness of the extremes of the "Women's Lib Movement" we should not overreact by condoning inequality.

In the 19th century, evangelicals were prominent in promoting equality for all. For example, Oberlin College, founded by evangelicals in 1833, became in 1835 the first college in the United States to admit black students on an equal basis with white students. Two years later, Oberlin was the first to admit women on an equal basis with men.

The organized women's movement in the United States began in 1848, a direct result of the fight against slavery. Quaker Lucretia Mott had been refused recognition as a delegate to the World Anti-Slavery Convention in London and came home to help found the women's rights movement. The two movements were thus tied together, and evangelicals fought for both.

Some of the same arguments given to defend slavery are being used today to defend unequal treatment of women. For example "slaves, obey" and "wives, submit" have been used by people who want to "Lord it over others." The overlords have forgotten the command that we are to submit to one another out of reverence for Christ.

As Mrs. Johnson said in her closing sentence, "Man's self-ishness, not God's plan, produced inequality." It is precisely for this reason that we must oppose the principle of inequality.

THE BIBLICAL VIEW of equality and the modern demand of equality for women are not the **AGAINST** same.

Christians sincerely want God's design for equality to prevail. But, the remedy is not found in the selfish measures being taken by the equality movement. The methods used to capture equality cannot be justified if those methods are opposed to biblical principles.

The Hebrew noun *ezer*, sometimes translated *helpmate*, means woman was made to correspond to man or be alongside him. She is neither subordinate nor superordinate. So Mrs. Rearick's argument that the 16 out of 21 times this noun is used in the Old Testament refers to a superordinate helper would lead us to believe that woman is superior to man. The superiority of woman over man is implied in some of the published material of the feminists movement. However, these 16 passages refer to God's help to mankind rather than to human relationships.

Jesus clearly teaches that we should look for ways to serve rather than ways to rule. But the social cry for equality emphasizes ruling over serving. The focus is on striving for "my" rights as opposed to an attitude of servanthood.

God has given us His Son and the Holy Spirit to provide us a way to attain the equality He designed. In this world Satan will try to influence us to seek equality through selfish means. God's plan for equality and the modern equality movement come from completely different directions. And they're bound for different destinations.

If we want to follow the teachings of God's Word, we cannot use selfish means to bring about equality.

1. Letha Scanzoni and Nancy Hardesty, *All We're Meant to Be* (Waco, Tex.: Word Books), 26.

2. Ibid., 34-35.

3. Patricia Ward and Martha Stout, *Christian Women at Work* (Grand Rapids: Zondervan Publishing House), 75.

4. Janet Smith Williams, Doctoral Dissertation (Conservative Baptist Seminary). Used by permission.

*Ann C. Rearick is a wife, mother, and church leader in her denomination.*

*Jamieline Johnson is a pastor's wife, mother, and Bible study leader in Kent, Wash.*

## Chapter 10

*The Issue:*

# Physical Fitness

*Statement for Debate:*

**Believers in the Lord Jesus Christ have a primary responsibility to maintain a high level of physical fitness.**

by

Millard Reed (For)

C. S. Cowles (Against)

*Background Scripture:*

**1 Corinthians 3:16-17; Philippians 3:17-19; 1 Timothy 4:7-8**

**W**HEN WE USE THE WORD *physical* in this debate we are referring to the human body that | FOR |

God created—a body He found precious enough to redeem, indwell by His Spirit, use, and which will one day stand glorified in His presence (see Job 19:26; 1 Corinthians 3:16-17; 6:19; 1 Thessalonians 5:23).

Fitness is to be judged on two bases: (1) pulse rate and (2) weight.

The pulse rate for a person who is physically fit will be no more than 72 beats per minute. (The rate for women may be 6 to 8 beats faster.)

A study by Dr. Jeremiah Stamler of Northwestern Medical School found that men with a resting pulse of over 80 beats were several times more likely to die from a heart attack than those with a pulse rate under 70. "Sudden death occurred 23 times as often for men with resting pulse rates over 80 and high cholesterol levels than for men whose resting pulse rates were below 70 per minute and with low cholesterol levels."[1]

The second factor in physical fitness is weight. There are several formulas for calculating proper weight, each of which is helpful. I suggest the one submitted by Dr. A. L. Heller in his book *Your Body His Temple*.

Women should multiply their height in inches by 3.5, then subtract 108. Next, they should measure their wrist. If the measurement is exactly 6 inches, your previous calculations have given you your ideal weight. If it is under 6 inches subtract 10%; if it is more than 6 inches add 10%.

Men should multiply their height in inches by 4, and subtract 128. Then they should measure their wrist and if it measures 6 to 7 inches, the weight is the same as the previous calculations. If it is under 6 inches, 10% is subtracted. If it is over 7 inches, 10% is added.

"Exercise? Exercise won't take it off—
Look at your double chin."

Life insurance charts reveal that for a person 10 pounds overweight at the age of 45, there is an 8% increase in chance of death. For a person 20 pounds overweight, there is an 18% increase; 30 pounds, 28% and 50 pounds, 56%.[2]

Along with a pulse rate that is 72 or less, a high degree of physical fitness calls for a weight that does not exceed the formula just listed.

*Maintain* is the key stewardship word of this statement for debate. If our pulse and our weight were uncontrollable factors, I would not argue their moral implications. But they are clearly and undeniably altered by faithful stewardship.

Regular exercise will lower the pulse rate. There are many alternatives for exercise programs. John Wesley ran each morning. Others prefer swimming, handball, or rigid walking. Dr. Roger Alteri, physiologist of our Nashville congregation, suggests the following formula: T.R. x 40 x 4. In order to have a fit and healthy heart, we should do any kind of exercise that accelerates our heart to our Target Rate. (Target Rate should be calculated by a physician. If the resting pulse is 80 it will be around 160 for ages 20-29; 153 for ages 30-39; 144 for ages 40-49; 139 for 50 and above.) We should continue that exercise for 40 minutes and do so at least four times a week.

By sensible eating habits we can bring our weight to within the maximum for which God designed us. Aerobic exercise has also been proved to be one of the best cures for obesity.[3]

In order to maintain physical fitness, it is also necessary to abstain from some substances. Beverage alcohol, tobacco, non-medicinal drugs, and refined sugar should be avoided.

A high degree of physical fitness, then, may be maintained through an exercise program that provides (1) a healthy heart with a pulse rate of under 72 and, (2) a sensible diet that assures proper weight, and avoidance of harmful substances.

Physical fitness is a "primary responsibility" because it increases the length and quality of life. You can add:

4 years to your life if you exercise regularly
5 years if you don't smoke
5 years if you practice weight control
2 years if you eliminate alcohol from your diet.[4]

This is more time for God to use us as responsible stewards. It cannot be a secondary matter.

It is also a "primary matter" because it is addressed by the scripture. "And they shall say unto the elders of his city, 'This our son is stubborn and rebellious, he will not obey our voice; he is a glutton and a drunkard'" (Deuteronomy 21:20, KJV). Joan Cavanaugh observes that the problem is not gluttony or drunkenness—they are mere symptoms. The real problem is stubbornness and rebelliousness.[5] Paul describes as "enemies of the cross" those whose "God is their belly, and whose glory is in their shame" (Philippians 3:19, KJV).

The portion of the statement for debate that is most severe in its implication is "believers in the Lord Jesus Christ." Each word in this triune title is significant.

We believe that Jesus is Lord. When He is Lord of the body that He created and lived in, it must be under His control (see 1 Corinthians 10:13).

We believe in Jesus. We believe that this very One who is eternal is also born of a virgin. We believe that He became acquainted with every temptation. He lived in a body like ours.

We also believe that Christ, the Living Word by whom the universe was created, also created our bodies and has power to control them.

Finally, we are believers in the Lord Jesus Christ, who made us and redeemed us and proposes to use us in our mortal bodies. We must maintain what He has created—and that maintenance is a primary responsibility.

E VEN THOUGH I average three to five miles a **AGAINST** day jogging, backpack extensively in the summer, and cross-country ski in the winter, I have a real problem with this statement for debate.

The issue is not that Christians should maintain good health. The issue narrows the physical fitness debate down to "a high level of physical fitness" and raises it to a position of "primary responsibility." My objections to this overstatement are as follows.

**1. It is discriminatory.** Where would Joni Eareckson and 32 million other disabled Americans fit into this scheme? Add to that those who suffer from deformity, disease, accident, or advancing age, and you have a vast number of people for whom the above resolution is not only impossible but even cruel.

**2. It is unbiblical.** The human body is held in high regard in the Scriptures as a marvelous creation of God. It is the temple of the Holy Spirit. It is not to be abused or misused. Curiously, however, there isn't one line in the Bible that even obliquely impels us toward maintaining a "high level of physical fitness."

To the contrary, the only place where the Greek word, *gumnasia* (exercise, disciplined activity) appears, it encourages quite the opposite: ". . . *exercise* thyself rather unto godliness. For bodily *exercise* profiteth little: but godliness is profitable unto all things, having promise of the life that now is, and of that which is to come" (1 Timothy 4:7-8, KJV).

**3. It distorts priorities.** It plays right into the hands of our culture's idolatrous obsession with the "body beautiful." In his article on "The Fitness Craze" *Time* magazine writer J. D. Reed observes, "The glorification of the body, the absorption with physical beauty, the passion for youthfulness and health . . . are transforming the nation's character, like it or not."[6]

He points out that Americans spend more than $30 billion on themselves toward the goal of attaining a "high level of physical fitness." That far exceeds what they spend on pursuing spiritual and aesthetic values.

Preoccupation with the physical self costs not only money but time and energy as well. Even modest programs of physical exercise or sporting activity eat up large blocks of time. In addition, they consume large quantities of not only physical but emotional energy that must be deducted from other important areas of life: family, devotional time, work, ministry to others.

For many it becomes a culturally sanctioned and ego-enhancing escape from essential responsibilities. Who takes seriously the complaint of a wife concerning her husband who devotes himself to an hour of running before work, two hours of tennis after work, golf and softball on the weekends, and who sleeps the rest of the time? And how about children who come home to an empty house while the mother is occupied at her aerobics class? Or their father who leaves his family behind and uses up his vacation time hunting, trekking, or mountain-climbing? Yet it is all justified because of the physical benefits gained.

**4. It detracts from the cultivation of the soul.** Preoccupation with the flesh tends to block out spiritual priorities. It obscures and even reverses the insight voiced by Paul when he said, "We look not at the things which are seen, but at the things which are not seen; for the things which are seen are temporal, but the things which are not seen are eternal" (2 Corinthians 4:18, NASB).

No matter how many laps we run or how many natural foods we eat, the time bomb of physical mortality relentlessly ticks away. It stands to reason that our priorities must be ordered by the fact that we are fundamentally spiritual beings destined to live forever.

This is not to say that concern for health and physical fitness necessarily wars against the soul—moderate activity may even enhance spiritual awareness. But it is important for us to realize that no physical enterprise can assume the level of a "primary responsibility" in the believer's life.

A close pastor-friend and his wife recently made a difficult but courageous decision: they quit running marathons. Why? Because it consumed too much time and energy. He found that his rigorous training schedule left him so depleted that he had little resources left to devote to sermon preparation and the necessary work of the church. His wife faced up to the fact that she was letting too many domestic responsibilities slide, not to mention opportunities for Christian service.

They still enjoy a good run early in the morning or late in the evening, and often take their teenage boys with them. Maintaining a high level of "physical fitness," however, is no longer a "primary responsibility." "We have found greater joy in both running and church ministry," they shared, "since we brought them back into proper balance."

We might paraphrase the question of Jesus in this manner: "For what does it profit a man if he maintain a high level of physical fitness and forfeit his soul? Or what shall a man give in exchange for his soul?" (Mark 8:36-37).

## Reaction and Rebuttal

C. S. COWLES IS CORRECT in the observation that the issue of this debate revolves around the interpretation of "high level" and "primary." We seem to agree that as Christians we should not abuse the body and that we should give it some degree of care.

FOR

But the fact is my opponent has sidestepped the central issue. He points out that some people become preoccupied with physical well-being and thereby neglect their families, their finances, or their soul. I have no wish to deny the fact that any good thing can be perverted. That is not the issue.

The issue is the stewardship responsibility that calls every Christian to give his maximum physical energies to God. It remains that excessive weight and lack of exercise reduces such energies and lessens the offering to God. Such a loss has serious moral implications because the responsibility for that loss rests squarely on the shoulders of the slothful and self-indulgent. Before God they are accountable.

That Cowles has conceded such a truth is reflected by the opening phrase of his first statement. His pattern of physical stewardship might serve us as a model.

I WONDERED, as I read Millard Reed's case, how the more than 1 billion people must respond who are uncertain about their next meal. I wondered how my grandfather might have reacted—all 260 pounds of him. His corpulent body did not fail him in 60 years of Christian ministry, including 20 years as a pioneer missionary to China. He died, alert of mind and sound in spirit, at age 87.

AGAINST

I wondered how a close pastor-friend would deal with this issue who, at 40 years of age, never takes a step without excruciating pain because of crippling rheumatoid arthritis. I won-

93

dered how that courageous student of mine would feel about Reed's case—a student who struggles from class to class in her cerebral palsied body?

I wondered why Moses did not think to add a command about physical fitness to the Ten Commandments, or why Jesus didn't devote at least a verse to its discussion in the Sermon on the Mount, or why Paul spoke candidly about his "thorn in the flesh" but never once mentioned pulse rate, weight, or exercise? I wonder . . .

1. A. L. Heller, *Your Body His Temple* (Nashville: Thomas Nelson Publishers, 1981), 45.

2. Ibid., 36-37.

3. Ibid., 64.

4. *Medical Tribune* (August 24, 1977), 46-47.

5. Joan Cavanaugh, *More of Jesus, Less of Me* (Plainfield, N.J.: Logos International, 1973).

6. *Time* (November 2, 1981), 96.

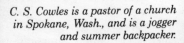

Millard Reed is pastor of a church in Nashville and is a systematic jogger.

C. S. Cowles is a pastor of a church in Spokane, Wash., and is a jogger and summer backpacker.

## Chapter 11

*The Issue:*

# Christians in Politics

*Statement for Debate:*

**Evangelical Christians should be actively involved in secular politics.**

by

Al Truesdale (For)

Clayton Bonar (Against)

*Background Scripture:*

**2 Corinthians 5:17-21; 1 Peter 2:13-17**

$T$HERE ARE TWO INESCAPABLE REASONS why Christians should become involved in secular politics.

| FOR |

For one thing, an evangelical Christian in a representative democracy has a moral responsibility to participate in secular politics. This is because in a democracy, participation is essential to the meaning and maintenance of a free society, as well as to the meaning of citizenship itself.

Unless a Christian is prepared to radically separate himself from life in the national community, and thereby forego all benefits that come out of a free society, then he must recognize that he is already a part of the vast governmental services and structures. This is the nature of citizenship in the modern democratic state.

Of course, a person may still say, "Well, I'm going to reap the benefits of citizenship, but I am not going to contribute anything." But "we, the people" is the fundamental premise of a democratic society. Practice of the art of politics is therefore viewed as a trust granted to stewards (politicians) by the sovereign people. The function of politicians becomes a representative one. They are to make laws and take actions that guarantee the republic's well-being. This means that all civil affairs, whether executive, legislative, or judicial, must serve the ends of human dignity for the whole citizenry.

In a democracy every citizen must exercise his gifts to insure social well-being, whether this be through the act of informed voting, productive employment, or by holding public office. All of these are ways by which citizens exercise their convictions about the nature of the state and political freedom.

No one can simply "dip in" to the society wherever he pleases—education, for example—and then condemn as evil or unworthy of Christian involvement that part of society

which he rejects—such as taxes. Such thinking simply displays an ignorance about the intricate nature of citizenship in a modern democracy.

The argument that politics is too often infested with corrupt people is certainly no argument against Christian involvement. Quite the contrary is true. How can a person who claims to be morally responsible trust the public welfare—national defense, education, administration of the nation's natural resources, taxation—to immoral, unprincipled stewards?

Here Plato's words are most appropriate, "He who refuses to rule is liable to be ruled by one who is worse than himself" *(The Republic).*

The second reason why evangelical Christians should be actively involved in secular politics is a religious one. Simply stated, it is that if we leave any part of life untouched by the grace of God, we undercut the claim that Christ is Lord.

We all believe that God became redemptively incarnate in Jesus of Nazareth. This means that Jesus actually became a part of this world where people seek an education, decide upon vocations, make decisions about where to live, and rear families. Here, in Jesus of Nazareth, the Incarnate God is present, walking city streets as carts and horses clamor by, where vendors hawk their wares, and where children play games. These are the same streets that carry people who must make political decisions and administer the affairs of state.

And why is He here? What is a holy God doing in such a place as this? Does He not thereby endanger himself or His reputation? He is here for one reason: to redeem it! How much of it? All that He created!

The New Testament says, and no responsible Christian can ignore it: "God was in Christ reconciling the world to Himself" (2 Corinthians 5:19, NASB). Is this true? Is His reconciliation actually this inclusive? If the New Testament is to be believed, the answer is *yes,* unequivocally.

Who are Christians and what is their purpose in life? They are people of this earth who have economic, political, domestic, and aesthetic dimensions to their lives that must be fulfilled if life is to achieve the fullness God intended.

Christians are simply people whose lives have come under the domination of God's grace. They know the meaning of restoration and reconciliation. And they declare that "where sin abounded, grace did much more abound" (Romans 5:20, KJV).

They neither approach the world as though God has turned over the major areas of life to perdition, nor as those who think some of the world is God's and some of it the unassailable possession of evil. Rather, they believe that the gospel of grace and human wholeness is addressed to every important aspect of life.

The political structures of society are certainly a very important part of our lives. And they are not left outside the intended impact and range of Christ's Lordship. True, according to the Constitution of the United States of America, no Christian has the right to impose Christianity on the civil order. But a Christian who holds political office can certainly bring the moral and religious strengths of the Christian faith to bear on the conduct of his office.

The Christian doctrines of creation and the incarnation of Jesus expose contempt for political participation for what it is: (1) a lack of faith in the transformative power of moral and religious conviction and courage; and (2) a sad misconception about the nature of God's relationship to His world.

Hᴏᴡ ɪɴᴠᴏʟᴠᴇᴅ should the conservative, **AGAINST** evangelical Christian be on the political battleground? We are, it is said, our own Caesar. We rule by ballot. And because of that, each man who holds franchise to vote should do so with conviction.

The real issue, however, is whether Christians should seek political office. I am persuaded they should not.

There are at least three overriding reasons why one might seek secular office. First, because of "the call of God—heeding the upward voice" in political life. If a man feels the call of God, who is to argue with him? Our history has had a number of men upon whom God laid the terrible burden of leading a nation.

But at best this is a risky premise to propose to a voting public, especially in our secular society.

Another justification for entering the political stream might be "the conscience—heeding the inward voice." One man's sense of right over another's seems to be the stuff of which campaigns are made. But to say one man is right because he is an evangelical does not resolve the issue.

Among quite conservative Christians who have spoken out on moral issues today are Dr. Billy Graham, who is in favor of a nuclear freeze, and Rev. Jerry Falwell, who opposes it. Both are men of conviction. Both are on opposite sides of an issue freighted with moral overtones.

We must also be aware that in the real politics of our democracy is the practice of compromise. Reality for the politician is supporting what his constituency wants. When the politician casts his vote, whose convictions is he supporting? If he does not vote the conscience of his public, and instead votes his own conscience, he is not a true representative. But if he votes their convictions when he disagrees with them, he will certainly have to compromise his convictions. Neither is a comfortable position.

It is made all the more difficult when we see that in most elections the vast majority of qualified voters do not even bother to go to the polls.

A third possible reason one would seek political office as a conservative evangelical would be "the convention—heeding the outward voice." It's the thing to do. Theologian Martin E. Marty suggests that the pendulum swing has recently been in the evangelical's favor. But he also suggests that the popularity of evangelical causes is not all that new. It just happens to be that the evangelicals are the ones who've been up to bat lately.

He reminds us that the very same things the conservatives were casting stones at the modernists for at the turn of the century (wealth, political clout, and social acceptance) are the same virtues evangelicals have sanctified for their own good today.

For these reasons today's evangelical has been called the "worldly evangelical" by some observers. His popularity has fostered a sense of pride of position rather than a spirit of genuine service to the populace.

Consider again the first reason one might enter political life. Sanctifying the civil office with a sense of divine calling still must stand the risks of a voting booth. The track record of such men and women has not been good enough for me to suggest either modern-day models or motifs to follow.

In the second option, heeding the inward voice, one must come to grips with the following logic: either all men in office today are of little or no conscience, or the laws on the books are not of sufficient moral vitality, or many good men of conscience in office today find themselves pressed to accommodate the conscience of others. I imagine the last is probably true. And this undercuts the argument for entering secular politics as an evangelical Christian.

Concerning the third option, I am not given to espousing a popularity vote for the evangelical. Men who run only with the favorable winds will scatter when the ill winds blow. This seems to be the weakest of all reasons for Christians to seek political office.

I see the role of the conservative evangelical to be a bearer of the good news of Christ. He is part of the church. And as such, his mission is spiritual. By subscribing to this premise we make a strong statement to our communities: the gospel of Christ is of primary importance. Such a statement makes a more effective impact in our world than an army of Christian politicians could ever hope to make.

Great Awakenings throughout history testify to the effects of authentic revival upon the social order. Homes were healed. Society was helped. Men and nations received new destinies.

The evangelical has this rich heritage to remind him of how best to impact his world. Ignoring the lessons of the past will diminish his striking force at the evils in our world. Voting booth politics is highly recommended. Christians should exercise their franchise. That, more than anything else, seems to shape the conscience of the politician. Not the other way around.

# Reaction and Rebuttal

First of all, Rev. Bonar nurses the illusion that it is *good* to exercise our franchise to vote, but it is *wrong* to serve as an elected official.

**FOR**

What logic is there in an evangelical Christian who supports the elective process by voting, then turns around and calls the elected office evil? And what is the morality of asking another person to do what you will not do yourself, or what you believe to be helplessly immoral?

We either support participatory democracy, or we don't.

Second, Rev. Bonar says a Christian politician would always have to vote according to his personal convictions—and because of this could not survive in the real political world. Because of the danger of compromise, he suggests the Christian should not serve as an elected official.

But this argument overlooks the meaning of "representative." Certainly at times an elected official must vote the will of his constituents even though he may disagree with them. At other times he may face irreconcilable conflict between the will of the people and his own deeply held moral convictions. In this case, he would have to vote his convictions. If the constituency is upset about this, they can vote him out of office.

Finally, Rev. Bonar says the Christian's mission is spiritual. This suggests that the gospel is of primary importance, and the political life of the community is relatively unimportant. But the truth is that a Christian in political office can affirm the importance of both. Senator Mark Hatfield has done this, and so has Senator B. Everett Jordan before him.

To say, as Rev. Bonar does, that a Christian should vote "with conviction," and then to double back and deny the potential for social improvement that can come through morally bold political leadership is to strip all meaning from the word *conviction*.

I would like to call your attention to three points on which both Dr. Truesdale and I completely agree:

**AGAINST**

1. Man is both social and spiritual in makeup.

2. Citizens have a moral responsibility to carry out their voting franchise.

3. The voting public is boss; politicians are the stewards.

Having said this, however, I must point out that my opponent missed the real issue here. The reasons for going to the voting booth are not necessarily the same as they are for seeking political office. In other words, because I believe in the free exercise of my vote does not mean I should run for office. Here Dr. Truesdale makes no real distinction. And this is crucial.

If he had made the distinction, Dr. Truesdale might not have used the above statements—on which we agree.

History has shown that where our nation stands among the nations most strongly is at the level of our trust in God—a trust that must be lived out, not legislated. The evangelical Christian may do anything he chooses, within the moral boundaries of the Holy Scriptures. But to say he *should* seek political office because he is an evangelical—well, thanks but no thanks.

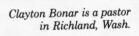

*Al Truesdale is an associate professor of philosophy of religion and Christian ethics at Nazarene Theological Seminary, Kansas City.*

*Clayton Bonar is a pastor in Richland, Wash.*

## Chapter 12

*The Issue:*

# Life-Support Systems

---

*Statement for Debate:*

**A Christian is obligated to use medical life-support systems.**

by

Della Blackburn (For)

Bob Mangum (Against)

---

*Background Scripture:*

**Genesis 2:7; Psalm 139:13-16; Philippians 1:21-24**

**M**EDICAL SCIENCE is continuing to introduce new procedures to doctors, nurses, and other **FOR** health professionals. These discoveries include drugs, therapies, and surgical techniques—all designed to conserve life.

In the light of these often phenomenal discoveries, what is the Christian's responsibility in using life-support systems? The obvious answer is that the Christian has an obligation to preserve the quality and, yes, the quantity of human life.

There are several reasons for using life-support systems.

1. We should respect the sanctity of human life. The basis of this principle is that *all* human life is of utmost value. God created human beings in His own image (see Genesis 1:26-27). And in love and compassion, Jesus Christ reinforced the worth of all people, including the disabled, diseased, and disadvantaged.[1]

2. The judgment that a person is incurably ill may be wrong. Medical opinion, no matter how knowledgeable, is never infallible.[2] How do we tell if such treatment will help the patient? The benefit, if any, is the continuation of life. Not preserving life is to destroy life—and to destroy life is to oppose the purpose for which God created life. In addition, to destroy life is to oppose the purpose of the medical profession—which is to promote wellness, to value life, and to protect life.[3]

3. The fact is, when we fail to use this means to prolong life, we support euthanasia.

Therefore, a Christian is obligated to use medical life-support systems to prolong life!

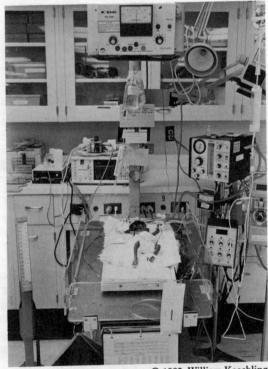

© 1985, William Koechling

What, then, is the problem? Why do we not always use life-support systems? Let's look at two reasons.

First, health care professionals are not all committed to the "sanctity of human life" principle. As a result, decisions are made on moral convenience rather than from a Christian point of view.

You can see a vivid example of this in the film *Who Should Survive?* made by Johns Hopkins University. The film shows how the medical staff and a family decided to allow a newborn with Down's syndrome and a blocked intestine to die. In an interview for *Christianity Today,* Dr. C. Everett Koop spoke of this case and said, "Mongolism is not curable, [but] the intestinal obstruction could have been fixed by a 20-minute operation, which has a 98 per cent effectiveness."[4]

Is there a difference between letting a patient die and hastening death? In an attempt to grapple with this, medical professionals have established guidelines for practice that feature terms as ordinary versus extraordinary means for preserving life and active versus passive euthanasia (mercy killing). But to bring these guidelines to life has been next to impossible. What was an extraordinary measure to preserve life yesterday is considered standard procedure today. And the term *euthanasia* has become a respectable part of our vocabulary that is used with the phrase "death with dignity."[5] But is allowing a newborn infant with Down's syndrome to starve to death (passive euthanasia) any more acceptable than taking an active step to terminate the life? In either case a willful decision has been made. And as Dr. Koop so aptly put it, "passive euthanasia is a cop out."[6] The word *passive* appears to be a term "more acceptable in the minds of those who commit such an atrocity than taking an active step to kill."[7]

A second reason we don't always use life-support systems is because of the active part legislators have taken in determining when and for whom medical life-support measures should be used. Many courtroom or other legislative decisions are made on the basis of age, social convenience, personal preferences, and even financial constraints rather than from sound moral principle—to say nothing of a biblical perspective.

The famous case of Karen Ann Quinlan is such an example. The Superior Court of New Jersey overruled the lower courts and granted the parents' request to withdraw the respirator that was thought to be sustaining the "meaningless life" of their daughter.[8] This decision and similar decisions are said to be in keeping with the individual's constitutional right to privacy and right to refuse treatment. The major concern is that such decisions will open the door for abuse of these rights, and the next step will be legalized euthanasia.[9]

A case in point was brought to the attention of the nation when Elizabeth Bouvia, a 26-year-old quadriplegic, requested to be allowed to die because she had "reached the limits of her potential and faced a life of pain and increased dependence on others." The newspaper quoted the physician as saying he would be "concerned about the legal implications and would welcome guidance from the court."[10] The physician should have had no question about the moral and ethical position of the case. He has clearly washed his hands of his responsibility and opened the door for further abuse.

What is the Christian's responsibility? May I suggest we uphold the dignity and sanctity of human life. This would take the kind of commitment that would say, "I know whom I have believed, and am convinced that he is able to guard what I have entrusted to him for that day" (2 Timothy 1:12). Look at it this way, because we believe God created man in His own image, He will guard and preserve the integrity of the individual. And so we must regard life as a gift from God. And we, too, must seek to preserve life—the life of the fetus as well as the life of the elderly. Human life is valuable regardless of the quality of life as defined by man.

I don't deny the dilemma we face when we have to make decisions in the midst of human pain. But we do have a solid base, a framework upon which we can operate. Such a position will provide hope to the Elizabeth Bouvias of this world, the same hope that led to Joni Eareckson Tada's triumph as described in her book, *A Step Further.*

Philip Yancey begins his book *Where Is God When It Hurts?* by expressing these thoughts: "I feel helpless around people in great pain. Really I feel guilty. They lie alone, perhaps moaning, their features twitching and there is no way I can span the gulf between us to penetrate their suffering. I can only watch. Anything I say seems weak and stiff."[11]

Discontinue life-support measures? Put them out of their suffering? Allow them to die with dignity? Is this the answer?

At the end of his book Yancey concluded with these words: "My anger [and] confusion about pain has melted mostly for one reason. I have come to know God . . . I am left with a solid faith in a Person which no amount of suffering can end."[12] His commitment was complete as a result of his commitment to Christ, not because he had become calloused to human pain.

In this day when our world is lacking an absolute ethical standard, be it resolved that we use all methods available to preserve the quality and, yes, quantity of human life.


As a general surgeon who has also done **AGAINST** my share of family practice, my experiences with life-support systems has been extensive enough to observe many remarkable results and some dismal failures.

There can be no question that blood and electrolytes lost in hemorrhage or dehydration from vomiting or diarrhea should be replaced. Neither can it be argued that a patient admitted to the acute coronary care unit of a hospital should not have all the support systems available. These may include insertion of a tracheal tube to make breathing easier, cardiac massage, and defibrillation, to restore heart rhythm.

In general, the medical profession has gone all out in using its resources to preserve life. To state, however, that a Christian is obligated to use life-support systems in all life-threatening situations is unreasonable.

I feel that before a person takes this step, several factors must be considered.

Before making a life-or-death decision, the first question I might ask myself is: *what is my obligation to God, who is my Creator and the Giver of life?* The concept that we are all made in the image of God is valid. But this does not necessarily mean, as some have said in recent publications, that a grossly deformed newborn infant with mental deficiency should be kept alive by many surgeries over a period of years.

Does God require this, or does He rather prefer a way of less suffering over the period of a few hours or days in the form of dehydration and hunger before the child returns to the Creator?

Or does God, in a different situation, demand that we continue life-support systems to a bedfast, nurse-dependent person who wants to leave this painful abode? I think not.

This brings me to my obligation to the patient, the recipient of the life-support systems. I might say that I deeply regret the widespread breakdown of the traditional doctor-patient relationship that enabled a physician to know the patient, often better than even family knew him. My obligation to this person is paramount. Anything that can relieve pain, give reassurance, and improve the condition of the acutely ill is my obligation.

Once the acute stage is past and the vital signs are stable, my continuing of life-support systems will depend on the type of brain or other organ damage. If my patient has had several heart bypasses, for example, and wants no further surgical intervention or heroic medical interference, I feel I should honor his request to discontinue support.

Another consideration is my obligation to the family. In the comatose patient—and even in the brain-damaged one who requires around-the-clock nursing care—my starting or continuing of life-support systems will depend on the patient's condition and the family involvement.

I do not believe the family and I are obligated to keep up life-support systems in many of these cases. There comes a time when the family, the minister, and the consultant, or family physician should decide to discontinue support and permit demise.

Patients who know they are dying must have support in the form of pain medications, expressions of love and concern, and symptomatic treatment.

Increased life expectancy brought about by marked improvements in diagnosing problems in unborns and infants, almost miraculous advances in medical care for the elderly, along with the invention and improvement of life-support systems, make the practice of medicine very complicated, to say the least.

In the case of the severely deformed, handicapped infant, obviously the patient involved cannot consent or refuse treatment. The family physician, consultant, pastor, and the parents must make the decision about whether or not surgery is desirable. This same group or committee could also serve a very useful purpose in determining whether or not to withdraw life-support systems.

I do not agree with those who would say that parents' decision is based primarily on emotions. If my child were born with a gross defect such as a completely ectopic heart (outside the body) or a severe spina bifida (opening in the vertibral column that exposes the spinal cord), I would think twice before subjecting my child to multiple surgeries and to all the pain and months or years of hospital care, with all that I know it entails.

Allowing a patient to die a relatively painless death by omitting life-support systems in selected cases is not cruel or thoughtless. Perhaps we should draw a sharp distinction between the euthanasia (mercy killing) of omission—which I feel is permissible in certain cases—and positive euthanasia by injection or other means. The latter cannot be morally justified. I feel this approach humanizes the issue.

I hope that by presenting the negative side of this issue I have stimulated you enough to encourage you to research the question more thoroughly. Many aspects of this problem cannot even be mentioned in this brief presentation.


## Reaction and Rebuttal

AFTER READING Dr. Mangum's argument, I've concluded we both agree that when we face a situation that centers around the issue of life-support systems,

| FOR |

the most important question we must answer is, "What is my obligation to God?"

Unfortunately, many Christians in medical crises ignore this question. They do this when they suddenly halt their search for God's direction. Just at the time when their Christian influence could make the greatest impact, they withdraw from the situation and turn over the decision-making power to those who are not committed to the sanctity of life.

Often, these decision-makers are people who don't even believe in the God in whose image we were created.

Let me conclude my argument with two questions.

1. As a Christian health professional, am I obligated to discontinue life-support measures simply because that is what the patient or family requests?

2. Or, is my most important responsibility to God?

My first and most important responsibility *is* to God. And when I live out this responsibility, I become to the patient, as well as to the family, a witness of hope and a reminder of the God of Creation.

THE BASIC REASON we use life-support systems is to respect the sanctity of human life. I **AGAINST** agree with this. However, I do not agree that using life-support systems is always beneficial to the patient or to his family. Neither do I agree that when we cease to preserve life, we are actually destroying it. God himself chooses not to prolong life in every case, even though we know He has that power. Therefore that argument is not valid.

In response to the quote of Dr. Koop, "passive euthanasia is a cop out," I would suggest a more accurate statement: "passive euthanasia may be a cop out."

Since accepting this assignment, a newborn was found in a local trash can. Though nearly dead, the infant was revived and kept alive by intravenous fluids and respirators for weeks. But primary and follow-up brain studies revealed no brain waves.

Here is a child without a brain, without parents—a burden to the state. Would keeping a child like this alive be an act of kindness? I think not. I believe that after emergency care and careful evaluation by a medical team, the merciful act would be to do nothing.

In conclusion, I'd like to say that Christian physicians and nurses find their greatest pleasure in helping bring a sick person back to health of mind, soul, and body. However, I believe there are exceptional cases in which parents, doctors, and ministers should make reasonable and morally responsible decisions to discontinue life-support systems.

1. NCR Staff, "This We Believe About Life and Its Value," *The Nurses Lamp* 32 (September 1980): 2-3.

2. C. E. Koop and R. A. Schaeffer, *Whatever Happened to the Human Race?* (Westchester, Ill.: Crossway Books, 1979), 57, 158-59.

3. NCR Staff, "This We Believe."

4. "Medical Ethics and the Stewardship of Life," *Christianity Today* (December 15, 1978), 11.

5. Koop and Schaeffer, *Whatever Happened?* 55.

6. "Medical Ethics," 13.

7. Koop and Schaeffer, *Whatever Hapened?*

8. T. A. Mappes and J. S. Zembaty, *Biomedical Ethics* (St. Louis: McGraw-Hill Book Company, 1981), 347.

9. Ibid., 367-73.

10. "Doctor Wouldn't Force-Feed Palsy Victim," *The Chronicle Tribune* (December 1983).

11. Philip Yancey, *Where Is God When It Hurts?* (Grand Rapids: Zondervan Publishing House, 1977), 11.

12. Ibid., 181.

*Della Blackburn is a registered nurse who directs the nursing program at Marion College in Marion, Ind.*

*Bob Mangum is a surgeon who lives in Nampa, Idaho.*

## Chapter 13

*The Issue:*

# Taxing Church Property

*Statement for Debate:*

**Church property should be taxed.**

by

Jerry D. Hull (For)

C. Neil Strait (Against)

*Background Scripture:*

**Matthew 22:15-21**

IDAHO'S Canyon County tax assessor's office lists 35,966 separate parcels of land.

**FOR**

The sizes of these parcels vary from small, half-lot house sites to large farms. Of this total, 1,766 are granted tax-exempt status. These exempt accounts include county facilities, city buildings, churches, colleges, grade schools, and numerous other charitable and nonprofit organizations.

We're not talking about "small potatoes" in Canyon County, Idaho, when we refer to the tax-exempt rolls. In fact, 1 out of every 17 properties does not produce tax revenue.

Many middle and upper class folk employ the words *parasite* or *leech* to describe welfare recipients. These words indicate that those with money believe some members of society are sponges that take, but never contribute.

The middle and upper class of our society are usually the ones who serve as leaders in voluntary organizations, such as churches. It is interesting to note that church leaders often place the church in the role of a taker, instead of the giver.

We propose that church property should be taxed. The following arguments provide sufficient reasons:

1. All recipients of essential services should pay a fair pro-rated amount. The term *essential services* implies different things to different people. For our argument, we will restrict, for the moment, this phrase to include only fire and police protection.

Focus on Canyon County. Why should 16 parcels of land be required to carry expenses for the 17th parcel? The essential services of fire and police protection are normally more difficult to provide for church properties than private residences because of the size and design of churches.

Perhaps the most unfair aspect of the nonpayment for essential services relates to the size of the land parcel. For example, my brother-in-law and sister live adjacent to a church that is one of the largest congregations in the county. They have a

nice home situated on a spacious double lot. They have only 260 linear feet of street frontage. Their property tax is $700 each year. In contrast, the church has about 1,250 linear feet of street frontage. The church pays zero dollars toward the county's $9 million annual budget.

2. Let's expand the definition of essential services to include more than fire and police protection. Every church I know gladly and readily pays its water and sewer bill, a service provided by local government. Above, we've established that, in the name of fairness, churches should also pay for the essential services of fire and police protection. There are many other essential services, however. For example: surfaced streets, traffic regulation markers, lighted street, planning and zoning commissions, code enforcement agencies, city management personnel, public schools, public parks, and the list goes on.

In my books, all of these are "essential services." All property owners, including the church, should share—and share equitably in these expenditures.

3. The church, more than any other segment of society, should support a healthy social environment. The church should be on the front lines of those willing to contribute to community coffers for the funding of social services. The church should model generosity in behalf of the needs of the community, especially since our modern era is marked by a stingy mood of curtailment. As a result of this mood, services to the elderly, poor, mentally ill, handicapped, school children, and many others have been reduced and reduced and reduced again.

Jesus showed great interest in the whole person and the whole social order. If the church carried its fair share of the tax load, there would a considerable larger "pie" to divide among the many deserving services and programs.

4. Why should nonbelievers and nonchurchgoers be required to pay for services provided for the church? Freedom of religion should allow people to deny supporting religion in any way, if they so choose. As it now stands, all taxpayers contribute to the support of church activities. This arrangement is "undemocratic."

5. Removal of tax-exempt status would help cut the number of nonorthodox, or "off the wall," religious groups. The current tax laws give a financial advantage to any group that wishes to file a charter as a religious organization. We, in the orthodox tradition, should attempt to protect the young and the easily persuaded from cultic and non-Christian influences that exist primarily for tax-exempt status.

We need not fear the increased financial burden of taxation. God will enable His Church to survive and prosper. He will give the church the ability to meet financial obligations, including this payment of property taxes. Why, then, do we perpetuate a system that makes it easy for nonorthodox and cult groups to exist?

Let's review the arguments that provide just cause for the church to pay property tax.

First, all recipients of essential services (fire and police protection) should pay a fair, prorated amount.

Second, the church should pay a fair amount of the costs for other community services.

Third, the church should take the lead in paying for services that contribute to a healthy social environment.

Fourth, nonbelievers and nonchurchgoers should not be required to pay expenses incurred by the church.

Fifth, removal of the tax-exempt status may restrict the number of cults and nonorthodox religious groups that exist within our communities.


THE DEBATE over taxing of church property is **AGAINST** not new. An early president, James Madison, raised the question. And D. B. Robertson, in his study of the question of taxation of church property, said that courts, lawyers, and church officials are still divided over the issue.[1]

I submit the following reasons as arguments against taxation of church property.

1. The church is service-oriented, and its very nature is giving. Hence, it returns to society something of more value than money.

Dean M. Kelley, in his book *Why Churches Should Not Be Taxed,* says, "The ministrations of churches are not advantageous to their members only but to the society as a whole, and are not merely advantageous to them but crucial for their collective well-being and indeed survival."[2]

Kelley adds, "Religion is entitled to special civil treatment, not just because it deals with the most intense and sensitive commitments of the human heart, but also because it performs a special function in society—one that is of secular importance to everyone—and its special treatment is the best way of insuring that that function is performed."[3] The end result of churches, according to Kelley, "is to help them [its adherents] 'make sense' of life."[4]

Dr. Jedediah Morse, writing on April 25, 1799, said, "To the kindly influence of Christianity we owe that degree of civil freedom and political and social happiness which mankind now enjoys."[5]

There is a strong historical thread supporting this truth. So much so that after hearing a case, the Supreme Court in effect declared that "tax preferences for churches are based upon long tradition and should, therefore, not be disturbed by federal interference."[6]

The force of history cannot be taken lightly. D. B. Robertson observes, "We do have a strong religious tradition. Even the officially and the genuinely irreligious apparently went along with the idea that religion is a good thing for the people and the country."[7]

2. Church taxation would mean an unfair double-taxation for those who support churches.

Dean Kelley wrote in a *Christian Century* article that "early rationale for tax exemption was that nonprofit organizations are simply not part of the tax base to begin with because their members already pay their own share of the costs of government as taxpayers in their own right."[8]

He further explains, "They would be taxed again for organizing themselves into groups for activities from which they derive no monetary gain and which indeed might also benefit the community."[9] Such taxation would "work to discourage . . . con-

116

structive endeavors so important to the health of a democratic society."[10]

3. A greater number of churches are involved in community-help programs and social ministries.

The churches, by the missions they perform, awaken the social conscience of the community. It is only logical to conclude that people who are inspired by churches help to raise the standards and safety of the society in which the people and the churches work.

Dean Kelley explains, ". . . over an extended period of time, and largely unconsciously, people derive from their basic framework of ultimate meaning a sense that it is right (or not right) to obey, affirm, and be loyal to a certain system of authority (or legitimated power). Without this sense of right-ness or legitimacy in the minds of most of the people, a ruler cannot rule; there are not enough policemen to keep an eye on everyone if the people are not to a large extent self-policing . . ."[11]

4. Churches and their constituents use fewer of some municipal services, such as the police, and do not appreciably increase the tax burden.

In *Why Churches Should Not Be Taxed*, Kelley concludes, "Genuine service charges are entirely different from paying a proportion of the whole municipal budget, which is not significantly increased by the presence of churches, and indeed might be greater if they were *not* there."[12]

5. The church exists strictly on a voluntary-giving principle. It is nonprofit. Heavy taxation would militate again the volunteer principle.

Taxation of volunteer giving concepts would stifle the involvement of volunteers and reduce the possible good that might accrue from the voluntary involvement. This kind of taxing would be a little like making people buy the right to do good.

6. Churches provide some services that communities would have to provide if churches did not exist.

By its very nature and mission, the church exists to perform services helpful to the physical, mental, and spiritual needs. But, as Kelley has observed, "Taxing non-profit schools and hospitals would raise the costs of education and medical care without any guarantee of a corresponding decrease in the cost of local, state or federal services."[13] The same would be true of churches.

7. The power to tax is the power to control. Perhaps this is the most valid reason not to tax church property. In Murdock vs. Pennsylvania, the courts ruled, "The power to tax the exercise of a privilege is the power to control or suppress its enjoyment ... Those who can tax the exercise of this religious practice can make its exercise so costly as to deprive it of the resources necessary for its maintenance."[14]

I submit these seven arguments against taxing of church property.

## Reaction and Rebuttal

I ENJOYED READING the crisp and thought-provoking arguments presented by my friend and worthy opponent, C. Neil Strait. Additional exploration of his arguments should help us clarify our thinking.

First, I agree the church should return to society something of more value than money, namely, Jesus and life in Him. This does not mean, however, that the performance of a worthy mission exempts the church from paying for the costs it creates for the city.

Second, the fact that churches have traditionally not paid taxes doesn't mean this should continue. Tradition simply records what has been done, which may have been wrong.

Third, the idea of double-taxation of churchgoers works two ways. In essence, nonchurchgoers are being double-taxed now. They pay the cost for their own property, plus a percentage more to cover the costs of the tax-exempt properties. Why should we deny nonbelievers the right to withhold support of churches?

Fourth, churches and their constituents may use more, not fewer, services. Church people may use the streets more (to and from church several times a week). What about the parks and city recreation facilities for children's parties and church ball leagues? The very nature of church buildings often require both specialized fire equipment and training. Stated simply, churches may be expensive organizations for any community.

Fifth, there is no documented evidence that taxation of churches would decrease voluntary giving. My review of church history suggests that the Church of Jesus has overcome every obstacle that has threatened to destroy its existence. The Church and its Lord are more than adequate for the local tax commissioners and any tax table they wish to follow.

T HAT SOME CONSIDER tax-exempt groups "parasite" or "leech" is not good rationale. This **AGAINST** may be neither factual nor fair. It borders on prejudice, rhetoric, and has nothing to do with the tax base.

Jerry Hull says church leaders "often" place the church in the role of a taker, rather than a giver. It is also true that "often" church leaders place the church in the role of the giver, rather than receiver.

Other arguments:

1, 2. "All recipients of essential services should pay a fair prorated amount." "Let's expand the definition of essential services to include more than fire and police protection ... for example: surfaced streets ... public schools." The fact is, participants in churches already pay a fair share. Should they be double-taxed?

3. "The church, more than any other segment of society, should support a healthy social environment." It does! The church, through ministries, creates a healthy society. The average person would not want to live where church ministries were jeopardized in order to maintain the tax structure.

That there would be a larger "pie" to divide among the service organizations is a diluted argument. Waste and corruption in these organizations negates this.

4. "Why should nonbelievers and nonchurchgoers be required to pay for services provided for the church?" The nonbeliever is recipient of the better society churches create.

5. "Removal of tax-exempt status would help cut the number of nonorthodox, 'off the wall,' religious groups." Not necessarily. Such organizations always find ways to skirt the law. To force them underground promotes devious life-styles.

1. D. B. Robertson, *Should Churches Be Taxed?* (Philadelphia: Westminster Press, 1968), 14.

2. Dean M. Kelley, *Why Churches Should Not Be Taxed* (New York: Harper & Row, 1977), 45.

3. Ibid., 47.

4. Ibid., 48.

5. Dr. Jedediah Morse, quoted by Verna M. Hall, comp., *The Christian History of the Constitution: Christian Self-Government with Union* (San Francisco: Foundation for American Christian Education, 1979), 68.

6. Martin A. Larson and C. Stanley Lowell, *The Religious Empire* (Washington/New York: Robert B. Luce Co., Inc., 1976), 9.

7. Robertson, *Should Churches Be Taxed?* 52.

8. Dean M. Kelley, "Are Tax Exemptions Subsidies?" *Christian Century* (June 9-16, 1982), 695.

9. Ibid.

10. Kelley, *Why Churches Should Not Be Taxed*, 11.

11. Ibid., 92.

12. Ibid., 96-97.

13. Ibid., 16.

14. Murdock vs. Pennsylvania, 319 U.S. 105 (1943).

*Jerry D. Hull is a dedicated churchman and dean of students at Northwest Nazarene College, Nampa, Idaho.*

*C. Neil Strait is the Michigan district superintendent for the Church of the Nazarene.*